What to Ask Your Accountant

ALSO BY THE AUTHOR

How to Manage Management

WHAT TO ASK YOUR ACCOUNTANT

A reference for those in business and those about to begin*

William E. Perry

*The small-businessman,
the self-employed,
and the individual

Beaufort Books, Inc. New York / Toronto

Copyright © 1982 by William E. Perry

All rights reserved. No part of this publication may be reproduced or transmitted in any form or by any means, electronic or mechanical, including photocopy, recording, or any information storage and retrieval system now known or to be invented, without permission in writing from the publisher except by a reviewer who wishes to quote brief passages for inclusion in a magazine, newspaper, or broadcast.

Library of Congress Cataloguing in Publication Data

Perry, William E.
    What to ask your accountant.

    Includes index.
    1. Accounting. 2. Small business—Accounting.
3. Self-employed—Accounting.
I. Title.
HF5657.P43   657'.9042   81-17094
ISBN 0-8253-0078-9   AACR2

Published in the United States by Beaufort Books, Inc., New York.
Published simultaneously in Canada by General Publishing Co. Ltd.

Printed in the United States of America   First Edition

10 9 8 7 6 5 4 3 2 1

Designer: Lucy Castelluccio

ACKNOWLEDGMENTS

THIS book grew from four influences on my life. First are those businesses that taught me the lessons incorporated in this book; second is Clement C. Chesko, Jr., of Guelcher, Chesko & Co., who recommended questions and areas to cover; third is Tom Woll, a super editor who tries ever so hard to make me look good; and lastly, my wife Cindy, who gave up the good life for three years while I did my accounting apprenticeship.

**Don't Criticize
Your Accountant's Judgment
—Remember Who Hired Him**

TABLE OF CONTENTS

Foreword	1
Section I—Organizing Your Business	5
Chapter 1—The Basics	7
Chapter 2—Going It Alone or Incorporating	17
Chapter 3—Setting Up the Books	31
Section II—Business Planning	51
Chapter 4—Financing the Business	53
Chapter 5—Establishing Plans and Objectives	66
Section III—Business Operations	81
Chapter 6—Living with Taxes	83
Chapter 7—Automating Systems	98
Chapter 8—Pricing Your Product	112
Chapter 9—Satisfying Regulatory Requirements	127
Chapter 10—Employees and Employee Benefits	142
Chapter 11—Surviving Cash Flow	157
Chapter 12—Controlling Record Keeping	172
Section IV—Analyzing Operations	187
Chapter 13—Constructing Financial Statements	189
Chapter 14—Putting It All Together	205
Appendix—Small-Business References	219

FOREWORD

When you get sick and consult a doctor, your primary concern is curing an illness. In addition, you normally ask for more information: you might inquire about a spouse's condition, a drug you have read about, or a magazine article you recently read on a medical topic. You look for a full-service doctor and keep pumping him or her for as much advice and medical insight as you can.

Now let's look at the typical consultation with an accountant (if you have one). You give him a bundle of notes and numbers, bid farewell, and await the results of his work. But there is something inconsistent here. Why don't you pump your accountant for financial information as you do your doctor? What about that new investment scheme you recently read about, the difficulties you are having collecting receivables from your customers, or the cash-flow problem you are concerned about? Are you aware of your accountant's skills? Or are you shy?

You may well be unaware of what your accountant can do for you, or perhaps you don't know what questions to ask him. This book contains many of those questions you shouldn't hesitate to ask.

ROADMAP THROUGH THE BOOK

This book is designed to assist you in utilizing your accountant's services. Its method is simple: a narrative section is followed by a series of questions for you to ask your accountant about each accounting service. Potential replies designed to help you both understand the question and evaluate the adequacy of your own accountant's responses are given in conjunction with the questions.

The book is divided into four major accounting service areas:

Section I. Organizing Your Business

New businesses or reorganizing businesses have strategies to design and problems to solve, including incorporation, establishing accounting records, and financing.

Section II. Business Planning

Businesses should do both strategic and tactical plannning. Strategic planning involves setting goals and objectives, while tactical planning develops the methods needed to accomplish the goals and objectives. When plans are in place, day-to-day decisions become easier because they either fit into the plan and are acceptable or are inconsistent with the plan and are rejected.

Section III. Business Operations

People live and become mired in the day-to-day operations of their business. To the small-business person there does not appear to be time for the other functions—only operations. Efficient and effective operations not only increase control and profitability but make time available for organizing, planning, and analyses.

Section IV. Analyzing Operations

You don't know who is winning the game until you see the score. Analysis involves the preparation and interpretation of financial statements, and both aspects are equally important. Properly used, the information contained in financial reports should help you restructure your operations to be more effective and profitable.

Section I

ORGANIZING YOUR BUSINESS

If you never do anything, you'll never do anything wrong—and you'll never do anything right.

CHAPTER 1
The Basics

IN THE beginning there were no budgets, financial statements, or government forms. People reaped the fruits of their labors and life was simple. People put their money in a safe place and whenever they wanted to know how much they had they just counted their tangible wealth.

Life was not destined to remain that simple. People needed to borrow money to expand businesses, buy homes, take vacations, pay debts, and so forth, and banks were reluctant to lend funds to a borrower who responded to the question, "How much do you earn?" with, "Enough," and then stated that their net worth was a half-full cookie jar. When governments decided to tax people on their earnings and began cranking up their printing presses to produce multiple-page tax forms, the record-keeping burden became unbearable. For seven days and nights the butcher, the baker, and the candlestick maker toiled in vain to tally their profits and net worth. By the end of the seventh day, factories ceased to produce because the staffs became bogged down in record keeping.

On the eighth day, God created the accountant, who proclaimed, "Go back to your jobs and leave the accounting to us."

THE ACCOUNTANT'S TRADITIONAL ROLE

Visualize yourself sitting at an average desk, in an average office, in the average manufacturing company. The door opens and in walks the head accountant. You can tell he is an accountant because

- He is dressed in a dark-blue suit, with a dark-blue tie, white shirt, and black wing-tipped shoes.
- The snarl on his face indicates there is no time available for small talk.
- He carries a large briefcase in which sharp pencils are neatly stacked, all the papers are in the right folders, and large, clean pads of paper are readily accessible.

He strides quickly to his desk, because accountants are almost never late, and if he is it's because he had an emergency at another client's. As the accountant prepares for the day's work, he draws from his inside pocket a forty-seven-key pocket calculator with 64,000 bytes of storage. He has consumed thirty-seven inches of adding-machine tape before nine a.m..

Your stereotype of an accountant might be slightly different from this, but you probably recognize most of the traits as similar to those your own accountant possesses. This book is about the man and the job—what your accountant can and can't do for you. Let's examine what most of us normally expect from our accountants:

- *Knowledge of accounting.* Obviously, we expect our accountant to know how to keep records, prepare financial statements, and explain, interpret, and advise us about those statements.
- *Knowledge of taxes.* We expect our accountant to know the tax laws, be able to complete any and all tax returns, and advise us on tax matters.
- *Production of accurate and complete work.* We expect the accountant to be a professional and to perform any and all accounting tasks accurately and completely.

We neither expect nor want to review the accountant's work to ensure its integrity.
- *Ability to keep me out of financial trouble.* We don't expect accountants to make financial decisions but we do expect them to alert us to tax-filing dates, poor accounting practices, and troublesome areas in our financial statements and to give us advice on the long-range implications of alternative financial choices.

While these expectations are valid, they have also led to a stereotypical image of the accountant that has caused many of us to underutilize this wizard of numbers. In the first place, the word "accountant" is often misused and misunderstood. Let's look at some of the different types of accountant:

- *Certified Public Accountant (CPA).* This individual is usually a college graduate who has passed a rigorous three-day examination administered by one of the state boards of accountancy, who has apprenticed under the auspices of a CPA, and who is licensed by the state in which he practices.
- *Chartered Accountant (CA).* The chartered accountant has the same qualifications as the CPA, and is the professional designation used extensively in Canada and in the United Kingdom and Commonwealth countries.
- *Public Accountant (PA).* If licensed, this individual has met state requirements to use the PA designation. In some states, the qualifications are rigorous, while in others anyone can use the PA title. Some states no longer use this title, but those individuals already possessing a PA can continue to use it. If your accountant is a PA, you should check your state's regulations as a means of determining the quality of training required for licensing. If your state does not

license public accountants anyone can use the designation; therefore it has no value.
- *Accountant.* This title is associated with an individual who does general accounting work, but the variety of jobs possible under such a title is so broad that unless it is qualified or described the designation's usefulness is doubtful.

Will the Real Accountant Stand Up, Please

All accountants help establish record-keeping systems and close and evaluate those records. Most prepare personal and business tax returns. Beyond these basic services the assistance provided by your accountant depends on his or her training, interest, and experience. In selecting an accountant you should look for a "full-service" individual.

Let's review the topics that our accountant can help with beyond those we normally expect:

Whether to go it alone or incorporate. One of the first decisions any business must make is whether to be under sole proprietorship or to incorporate. The accountant works with both forms of business, knows their advantages and disadvantages, and is in an excellent position to advise on such a matter.

Setting up the books. Record keeping is an essential but time-consuming part of all businesses. Let your accountant design a cost-effective record-keeping system to minimize your efforts and maximize the available financial information for your analytical use (see Chapter 3).

How to finance the business. Banks are always anxious to lend money to businesses that don't need funds but are hesitant to provide cash for the needy. Accountants can sometimes help with arm twisting at the bank, as well as with advising you on other sources of funds (see Chapter 4).

Establishing plans and objectives. If a business doesn't know where it is going, it won't know when it gets there. Planning is essential. Accountants have the opportunity to observe methods of planning and the results of both good and bad planning. While the accountant's specific expertise is financial, he can help organizations develop realistic business plans (see Chapter 5).

How to live with taxes. Pity the poor business person who waits for the end of the year to find out how much tax is owed. You can influence your tax bill—and your accountant can help you—if you take appropriate steps before the end of the year (see Chapter 6).

Automating systems. The question is not whether a computer is needed; the question is when and how to use it. The cost of the equipment is insignificant compared to the cost of use and to the potential benefits. Work with your accountant in deciding how automation can help your business (see Chapter 7).

Pricing your product. Few organizations stay in business when they sell their product for less than cost, and yet many businesses are unsure of what the exact cost of their product is. Let your accountant make sure your revenues are greater than your expenses each time you sell a product (see Chapter 8).

Satisfying regulatory requirements. One of the jobs businesses learn quickly is that of filling in and filing the ubiquitous federal, state and local forms. Failure to file or to comply with the numerous regulations leads to fines and other sanctions. No business to date has made a profit by spending time filing federal forms; do what you do best—run the business—and let your accountant complete the forms (see Chapter 9).

Employees and employee benefits. Employees have personal responsibilities, problems, complaints—and an insatiable desire for more money. To be effective, a business must respond to all of these matters. Salary is only part of the wage package: it is not uncommon for benefits to equal or exceed twenty-five percent of the total wages, and most of those benefits are regulated by law. Have your accountant help your employees, and you, benefit from employee benefits (see Chapter 10).

Surviving cash flow. It is possible to be profitable and go bankrupt. Without sufficient inflow of cash to pay current bills, businesses are in trouble. Let your accountant project and work with you on improving your cash flow (see Chapter 11).

Controlling record keeping. Financial control is an important part of the managerial function. If your accountant is not well versed in this area, look for a new accountant (see Chapter 12).

Constructing financial statements. Both the government and the owner want financial data properly recorded. Improper recording may lead to wasted—or embezzled—funds. When revenues and expenses are sorted and added, your accountant will present you with a series of financial statements. They must supply relevant information you need and you must know how to use it. Work with your accountant to interpret and improve your financial reporting (see Chapter 13).

Putting it all together. Accountants come in all sizes and shapes. Some can even do things other than accounting. Every so often you must sit back and ask yourself if your business is successful and, if so, where you want to take it. Don't overlook ways in which your accountant can help expand your operations, improve profitability, and consider new ventures (see Chapter 14).

How do you know if your accountant can do all these things? That is what this book is all about. It is designed to help you receive maximum benefit from one of your most valuable resources—your accountant. Use the questions in this book to build a new working relationship with him.

MANAGERIAL VERSUS ACCOUNTING DECISIONS

You may, while reading this book, get the feeling that your accountant should be running your business. This is not the intent of the book. You as owner and manager of your business should run it and make the necessary managerial decisions about the why, how, when, where, and who of it. On the other hand, two of the tools to help you are your accounting system and your accountant. Decisions on the type of books you should keep, the methods of recording transactions, financial analyses, tax planning, and the preparation of returns and financial statements are accounting decisions. You may wish to rely on your accountant's judgment for these.

No one knows your business better than you, and no one has more invested in the business than the owner-manager. Use your accountant as a resource, *but* you should do personally what you do best and let your accountant do what he or she does best.

SELECTING AN ACCOUNTANT

You should select your accountant carefully, using a rigorous process. The accountant is too important to your business to leave the choice to a subordinate. The process described below to assist the chief executive officer in selecting his organization's accountant examines the accountant's technical, professional, and interpersonal skills.

Step 1: Develop A List of Candidates

The screening process begins with a search for potential candidates, which can be obtained from:

- friends and acquaintances.
- business associates.
- professional advertising.
- professional brochures and publications.
- state or provincial accounting associations.
- professional associates such as lawyers and bankers.

Unless unusual conditions exist in your business that require specialized accounting skills, the candidates should be from the local area. This will reduce the accountant's expenses, and he will only have limited travel costs, and home office support will be readily available to him if needed.

Step 2: Narrow Down the List of Candidates

Initial investigation of the candidates should indicate the best and most respected accountants in your community. You should not pay to train an inexperienced accountant. Those whose credibility is difficult to substantiate should be dropped from the list.

Step 3: Verify the Accountant's Availability and Capability

Determine your accounting requirements. You can establish what types of services you may need by reviewing the areas of potential accounting assistance outlined in this book. Discuss informally the accountant's ability to provide the necessary services and his ability to provide them personally. Look for a specific individual, not a firm. The firm may have time for your account, but the individual may not.

Step 4: Interview the Candidate

Specify the desirable professional and personal traits you want to find in your accountant. (With the exception of interpersonal skills, desirable professional traits will be reviewed in this book.) Remember that in addition to his professional responsibilities the accountant is your financial counselor. You must have confidence in him so that you will be willing to follow his advice. It makes no more sense to go to a medical doctor and receive advice that you ignore in preference to home remedies than it does to work with an accountant and then fail to follow his financial advice.

The interview must be probing and cover the following points:

- Does this individual have a personality I can work with?
- Can this individual provide the services I need?
- Can this individual provide services when I need them?
- Does this individual have the needed skills and experience to do my work effectively, efficiently, and economically?
- Can this individual's organization properly support him?

Step 5: Cost

The last step in the selection process involves economics. Accounting fees vary between twenty-five and several hundred dollars per hour, depending on the individual and the firm. Small local accounting companies are usually less expensive than the national firms, but don't depend on it until you check. There are three types of quotes your accountant can give you:

- *An hourly rate.*
- *A fixed fee.* A predetermined fee for a specified service, such as X dollars for preparing your tax return.
- *A competitive bid.* You describe the desired services and then request bids for the job from two or more accountants.

Step 6: Contract for a Small Service

When you have selected the one or two accountants who you feel would be most appropriate for your business, engage them for a small service such as preparing a tax return or reviewing financial statements; or ask them to recommend improvements in a troublesome area of your business. The objective of contracting a small job is to test an accountant's skill, service, timeliness, and cooperativeness prior to engaging him on a full-time basis. The small investment normally pays dividends.

Step 7: Award the Contract

If you are pleased with the service received, fees stated, and your working relationship with the accountant, engage that individual on a full-time basis. Obviously, if the accountant performing a special task does not fulfill your expectations don't allow him to continue. Begin the selection process again.

IS THE SELECTION PROCESS WORTH IT?

Many small businesses choose accountants for the wrong reasons. Few make a methodical search. Normally they spend more time selecting an automobile than an accountant, even though the consequences will be far greater with the latter. The baker does the baking, but you can tell a good loaf of bread from a bad loaf. A carpenter builds, but you can distinguish a well-framed home from a poorly framed home. A secretary types, but you can tell a well-typed letter from a poorly typed letter. Why then shouldn't you be able to distinguish a good accountant from a bad accountant? Put the same time and resources into selecting your accountant as you do in making other significant decisions.

CHAPTER HIGHLIGHT

Selection of the right accountant can help increase your profitability—not by increasing sales but through the evaluation, management, and reduction of costs. Don't underestimate the value of a good accountant.

CHAPTER 2

Going It Alone or Incorporating?

ONE of the most momentous decisions an individual makes is to form his own business. The experience parallels other critical experiences in life: you can read about them, and you can talk about them, and you can plan to do them; but until you have gone through the agony and the ecstasy it is impossible to adequately describe them. Going into business for yourself, like other major decisions, should not be undertaken hastily.

WHY SMALL BUSINESSES FAIL

It may appear inappropriate to discuss why businesses fail before explaining how to organize the business. However, the topic is germane because the organizational process itself can affect the probability of business success or failure. Furthermore, the causes of business failure must be understood before they can be adequately addressed during the organizational process.

Many small businesses are doomed before they open their doors. The majority fail within two years, primarily for the following reasons:

Inadequate planning. The business selects the wrong location, wrong product mix, prices its product poorly, does not have adequate capacity or ability to satisfy user demand, or has inadequate quality standards. In other words, the business offers the wrong product, in the wrong place, at the wrong time, or for the wrong price.

Underfinancing. It takes time to get a new business going. If sufficient funds are unavailable to carry the business during the start-up period, it may run out of cash before it has had sufficient time to become established and generate a profit.

Insufficient information. Information is the lifeblood of most organizations. Businesses need to know whether they are making or losing money on their sales, when to reorder, when customers' accounts become delinquent, when to file federal forms, plus a myriad of other pieces of data needed to drive the business. If this information is unavailable, the manager must make decisions based on intuition. Bad business judgment not only affects profitability but may cause still other poor decisions to be made. While proper information does not guarantee success, it increases its probability.

Improper organizational structure. Businesses normally involve many people. The organizational structure selected must satisfy the key personnel and provide the necessary flexibility to keep these people happy while providing for continuity and growth. Improper organizational structure can result in extra record keeping, additional taxes, and disputes among the principals.

ORGANIZATION STRUCTURE CONSIDERATIONS

The three recognized classes of business are sole proprietorships, partnerships, and corporations. Each has its own legal characteristics and each has advantages and disadvantages for the owners. If you want to be in business, you must select one.

Sole proprietorship is the simplest organizational form. A person says, "I'm a sole proprietor" and he is one. Dissolution of a sole proprietorship is just as simple. This is the structure for the person who does not want to undertake any organizational expense or extra paperwork. Its advantage is simplicity; its disadvantage is direct legal and tax liability. Business debts and liabilities are the owner's debts and liabilities, even if the business ceases operations.

The partnership is a multiowner organization also without benefit of the tax advantages of corporations. The main reason for forming a partnership is to ensure that those involved are personally liable for their actions, which is a requirement in some professions. The major disadvantage of a partnership is that each partner assumes liability for the actions of all other partners.

For most small businesses the question is whether to choose sole proprietorship or a corporation. The creation of a corporation is the equivalent of the birth of a new individual. Under law, the corporation is an entity unto itself and is treated as such. Once the corporation is created it is difficult to terminate. The business functions, such as purchasing, contracting, and hiring employees are considered to be performed by the corporation and not by the individual working for the corporation. Thus, while the corporation eliminates personal liability and offers tax benefits, it also creates extensive paperwork.

Criteria for Deciding Organizational Structure

Examine the following cases where someone made the wrong decision:

Case A. Too much paperwork. Mary wanted to start a part-time business selling products on commission. A good friend recommended she incorporate as Mary's Cosmetics, Inc. She did. As a corporation, Mary was required to file local, state, and federal corporate tax returns. The paperwork was so extensive that she needed to hire an accountant, which consumed a large part of her profits. Later, Mary decided to stop selling, but the corporate paperwork had to continue, even though there was no income.

Case B. Dispute among the principals. Bill and Mike started a small print shop. Being good friends, they created a partnership. Business ballooned, but eventually Bill felt that Mike was not carrying his share of the load. Disputes grew until continuing the business was intolerable to both partners. Neither wanted to sell to the other, however, so they sold off their assets and divided the funds. They had not prearranged a method for dissolving the partnership and maintaining the business.

Case C. No place to hide profits. Jack was a struggling author, working during the day and writing at night. He operated his business as a sole proprietorship and filed his tax returns accordingly. Jack's book sales began to blossom, and overnight he began raking in more money than he ever dreamed possible. In no time, he was paying the maximum income-tax rates—easy come, easy go, without the benefit of corporate tax shelters.

The organizational structure decision rests with the owner. In making that choice, he should consider the following criteria:

Tax avoidance. The organizational structure can be designed to avoid the payment of unnecessary taxes. It is possible to establish corporate benefit plans that defer or avoid taxes; at the same time there may be corporate taxes to pay that would not be incurred under a sole proprietorship. The amount of profit, future investment, the number of employees, and a desire to give to employee benefits are all tax factors that should be considered when determining the structure of the business.

Liability. The corporate structure is an entity by itself and is thus liable for its actions. On the other hand, the corporation does not protect the individual from certain kinds of liabilities, improper acts or acts not authorized by the corporation. The type of business is a factor in personal-liability organizational-structure considerations.

Allocating control. The corporate structure provides advantages in allocating control of an organization among a number of people. Through issuance of stock it gives the option of control to anyone with the means to purchase a block of shares large enough to control the board of directors. The sole proprietorship puts control of a business in the hands of one owner. The desire to retain direct control or allocate control of the business is an organizational consideration.

Continuity. The sole proprietorship ceases along with the sole proprietor. The corporate structure, as an independent entity, has an unlimited life, which allows for easier transfer of control (assuming the business is desirable to another party).

Buy-out versus dissolution. The sole proprietorship can be dissolved much more easily than can the corporation. On the other hand, the corporation offers some advantages in the transferral of control, for example the sale of stock transfers ownership in a corporation. While most business people are reluctant to discuss going out of business at an organizational meeting, when more than one person is involved, establishing the method of dissolution or buy-out while the partners or stockholders are on friendly terms simplifies the process when problems occur.

Raising capital. The key to raising funds for a business is the stability and ongoing nature of the business as well as its current worth. The corporate structure offers more options than the sole proprietorship or partnership for raising capital, such as the issuance of stock and/or commercial paper.

CHAPTER HIGHLIGHT

Understand your own business organizational needs and then select your organizational form.

QUESTIONS ABOUT TAX AVOIDANCE

If tax avoidance is an organizational consideration, you may want to ask your accountant the following questions:

QUESTION: What type of corporate benefit plans can I establish to help avoid taxes?
CONSIDERATIONS: A corporation permits you to implement employee benefit plans such as life or health insurance, pension plans, and so forth for the benefit of you and your employees. However, you must take into consideration that liberal benefits, which would be to your advantage and which would lower taxes, must also be provided to your employees. Benefit plans will cost money to establish and operate and in some instances become almost a permanent commitment of corporate resources (both financial and administrative).

QUESTION: If I decide to establish my business as a sole proprietorship, what benefit plans can I establish to avoid taxes?
CONSIDERATIONS: Employee benefit plans are available to the sole proprietor but are normally more limited in scope than those available to the corporation. Normally, through a Keough or Individual Retirement plan the sole proprietor is permitted to invest a limited amount of his profits into a tax-free retirement plan. The tax, as with the corporate retirement benefit plans, is actually deferred and becomes payable at the time the retirement benefits are distributed.

QUESTION: What are the tax advantages and disadvantages of incorporating?
CONSIDERATIONS: In a sole proprietorship, profits are included as the proprietor's personal income and are taxed as ordinary income. The corporation, on the other hand, being a separate, distinct entity, is taxed as such and its profits are then distributed to its owners as dividends. Dividends (after a small federal exclusion) are taxed as ordinary income. With proper financial records, it is possible to gain tax advantages through increased benefit plans. There are methods—such as declar-

ing bonuses—that give corporate earnings to the owners and effectively—and legally—let the corporation avoid paying taxes by reducing its pre-tax profits. In order to declare the proper bonus, exact records must be maintained so the owners know the profit of the organization prior to the end of the corporate tax year.

QUESTION: Would a subchapter S corporation provide me the same tax benefits as a regular corporation? (A subchapter S corporation provides corporate-liability protection, but corporate income is treated as the personal income of the owners. Consequently, the corporation isn't taxed as a corporation for income-tax purposes.)

CONSIDERATIONS: From a legal viewpoint, a regular corporation and a subchapter S corporation are the same. They are both legal entities under the law. The only differences relate to taxation. The income derived from the subchapter S corporation is treated as ordinary income of the corporation's owners. Thus, the subchapter S corporation pays no corporate income tax. In addition, there are limits on some of the benefit plans that can be established by a subchapter S corporation. (The U.S. Internal Revenue Service has a brochure on subchapter S corporations.)

QUESTION: If I establish corporate benefit plans, must I contribute to those plans in the corporate taxable year?

CONSIDERATIONS: The corporate contribution to most benefit plans must be paid within the taxable year in order to get the deduction for the contribution to the plan. However, some retirement plans are treated differently. In certain circumstances, the law permits both advanced and deferred payments to a pension plan. Thus, if a corporation had very high profits in one year it could make extra contributions to a pension plan, within the pension restrictions of course, and in lean years defer the contribution for an extended period of time. Discuss this option with your tax counsel to identify the qualifying conditions.

QUESTION: What is the best way to pay for property and equipment if I take all the money out of the corporation at year end to avoid paying corporate income tax? (This applies primarily to family-owned corporations.)

CONSIDERATIONS: If you buy plant and equipment with corporate funds, you normally cannot deduct the full amount as business expenses in the year in which you make the purchase. The cost of the purchase may have to be depreciated over several years. You may not have cash available to pay for the equipment if you give all of the profits to yourself through salary or bonus. However, you can buy the plant and equipment personally, and then rent it back to the corporation, subject to certain tax restraints. (See the current IRS brochure on leasing to corporations.) This approach enables you to withdraw all of the profits from the corporation so that you are only taxed once.

QUESTION: Who gets the investment tax credit when a corporation buys plant and equipment?

CONSIDERATIONS: An investment tax credit is a dollar-for-dollar credit against tax due for up to 10 percent of the purchase price of equipment in the year of purchase. (See IRS brochure on investment tax credit for current information.) In order to gain an advantage from the investment tax credit, it is necessary to have a profit. If all of the funds are withdrawn from the corporation, there will be no profit against which to apply the investment tax credit. Therefore it may be advantageous to buy property personally and rent it to the corporation, so that you as an individual can gain the tax advantage of the investment tax credit. Also, if you are in a higher tax bracket than the corporation you will gain more tax advantage by taking the tax credit personally. Note that if you are a sole proprietor you can deduct the investment tax credit from your personal income, even though your business loses money.

QUESTION: Do the tax laws regarding incorporation vary depending on the state or province in which the incorporation occurs?

CONSIDERATIONS: Each state or province has its own laws regarding incorporation. While the laws may be similar, there are some significant differences that may affect the method of filing, the method of reporting, the number of owners required for incorporation and in some instances may place restrictions on the business activities. There can also be significant tax considerations in different states. Also, if a corporation is formed in one state or province and desires to do business in another state or province, it may be required to file as a foreign corporation within the other state or province and pay tax as a foreign corporation.

QUESTIONS ABOUT LIABILITY

The business person with organizational questions about personal liability within the business should ask his accountant the following questions:

QUESTION: Will a corporate structure limit my personal liability for business transactions?
CONSIDERATIONS: In some lines of business, notably manufacturing areas, liability for defective products and so forth is limited to the resources of the corporation. In other types of businesses, particularly those dealing with personal services, liability is not affected by whether the individual is a sole proprietor or works through a corporation. In other words, if an individual holds himself to be an expert, such as a tax advisor, he cannot limit his personal liability to the assets of the corporation.
QUESTION: Should I consult a lawyer about my personal-liability concerns?
CONSIDERATIONS: In order to become certified, an accountant must take some basic courses in business law and prove his competence. An accountant, however, is not a practicing lawyer and therefore cannot answer technical legal questions. In most instances, the accountant would decline to provide legal advice. The accountant should be able to recognize when it would be wise to obtain legal counsel.

QUESTIONS ABOUT ALLOCATING CONTROL

If you are concerned about the control of your business (and you'd better be), you should ask your accountant the following questions:

QUESTION: If I incorporate, how do I retain control of the corporation?

CONSIDERATIONS: The corporate structure involves the issuance of stock, which represents ownership. The founders of the corporation usually buy the shares of corporate stock that represent their majority ownership in the corporation. However, when the corporation is formed, there are X number of shares available. Normally all of those shares are not issued; some, called treasury stock, are retained for a later time. Should the founders want to raise money, they can sell this stock; should they want to provide incentive for the employees, they can offer a stock-option plan; or they can purchase more shares themselves as a way of changing their percentage of ownership of the corporation.

QUESTION: Are there other ways of letting people control corporations besides issuing stock?

CONSIDERATIONS: The real control of a corporation is through stock ownership. But, employees can be appointed to corporate-officer positions so they have authority and control in the day-to-day operation of the organization. Since they would report to a board of directors they do not exercise ultimate control—they can be fired.

CONTINUITY QUESTIONS

Founders of businesses who have questions on the continuity of the business should ask their accountant the following questions:

QUESTION: What happens to a small business when the proprietor can no longer continue running the business?

CONSIDERATIONS: The sole proprietorship is owned by the individual. If someone else were to officially take over the business as owner, a tangible asset has changed hands. The effect of transfer of ownership is that the proprietor or his family may no longer be involved in the business; if they are, they will serve at the pleasure of the new proprietor.

QUESTION: Does corporate organization support the continuity of the business?

CONSIDERATIONS: A corporation provides alternative means for transferring ownership from one party to another, thus facilitating continuity of operation. Three options are available for passing along control of the corporation: the owners of stock can sell it; employees can be offered stock-option purchase plans, which over a period of time permits them to buy control of the corporation at minimal prices; the unissued shares of the corporation can be offered at a public sale, permitting employees and the public to buy control of the corporation. Once a market for the stock has been established, the original owners can sell the remaining shares.

BUY-OUT-VERSUS-DISSOLUTION QUESTIONS

If the organizers of a business are concerned about its dissolution, the following questions can be directed to their accountant:

QUESTION: Should the organizing process include contingency plans for the dissolution of the business?

CONSIDERATIONS: Yes. If more than one party is involved in the business, the method of dissolving it should be determined during the origination process. Attempting to dissolve a business when the parties are feuding is a difficult, time-consuming, and costly process. Even in marriages of people with substantial wealth, it is common to spell out before the marriage occurs the distribution of that wealth in the event of a divorce.

QUESTION: What methods are available to dissolve a business?

CONSIDERATIONS: There are as many ways to dissolve a company as one's imagination can contemplate. The two most common are to sell off the assets of the business and divide the proceeds in accordance with a predetermined distribution formula, or to sell the business itself on the open market and divide the proceeds. The selling of the resources is normally the quickest of the two methods. The real problem is the distribution of the proceeds among the owners. It is important that the distribution method be spelled out clearly.

QUESTION: Could the dissolution process provide for a buy-out by one party?

CONSIDERATIONS: The buy-out option is reasonable, but terms must be specified ahead of time. The reason for this is that when such a time comes, neither party may have or be able to borrow sufficient funds to buy out the other owners. If the method of buy-out lets the process occur over a period of time, it is much more likely to succeed.

QUESTION: Are there taxes involved when a business is dissolved or when one partner buys out another?

CONSIDERATIONS: There is a tax on the increased value of the business above that value recorded on its books. The increase in value is taxed at the capital-gains rate as opposed to the income-tax rate.

QUESTION: Are these funds taxable as ordinary income?

CONSIDERATIONS: The tax considerations depend on the type of organization, the length of period the assets have been held, and the method of selling those assets to the buyer. Tax questions are very complex and need to be carefully considered before a business is sold. The wording of the purchase agreement and the method in which the sale is conducted can affect the tax liability of the seller. If the method of selling the business is not agreed upon during friendly times, one or more of the sellers may not be willing to make concessions to minimize the tax liability.

QUESTIONS ABOUT RAISING CAPITAL

If it becomes necessary to raise capital, ask your accountant the following:

QUESTION: What type of information will I have to present to lenders before I can raise capital for my business?
CONSIDERATIONS: People who lend money have three primary considerations. First, they want to know what type of assets or collateral you have to borrow against. If you have established your business as a corporation, then their interest is in the assets of the corporation; if you have established your business as a sole proprietorship, the primary concern is your personal assets. Second, they are interested in the skills, capabilities, and track record of the owners. If you are well respected in your business, the bank would be more willing to lend you money than if you are a novice. Third, they assess the potential of the business. If it is a high-risk venture, such as a restaurant, they would be less likely to lend money than if it is a low-risk business.
QUESTION: If I am a sole proprietor, how can I borrow funds without risking the loss of my personal assets?
CONSIDERATIONS: The extent of your risk when you borrow funds depends on what you pledge to cover those funds. The wording of the loan agreement is extremely important if you are concerned about loss of your personal assets. If such loss is a major concern to you, you should probably consider incorporating and then borrowing through the corporation.
QUESTION: Will the existence of a corporate structure help me raise funds?
CONSIDERATIONS: Purchasers of stock in small businesses have the same three considerations as bankers. But the corporate structure offers the opportunity of raising capital through the issuance of stock. Purchasers of stock have a different type of collateral, one that offers them the opportunity for capital gain if the business is successful. On the other hand, the banker's

profit is limited to the amount of interest charged on the loan. The extra incentive of ownership and capital gain may encourage investors to accept more risk while providing you with needed capital.

QUESTION: What type of financial statement is necessary as preparation for raising capital?

CONSIDERATIONS: The two financial statements of interest to most investors are the balance sheet and statement of income and expense. If it is a new corporation, you will be able to prepare a balance sheet but will not have had any income and expense experience. In that case prepare a statement of estimated income and expense for the next few years to encourage lenders to provide funds. Other statements of interest to investors would be lists of potential customers for your business, lists of contracts in hand, and a cash-flow projection that shows you will have sufficient capital to survive until your business is financially self-sufficient.

QUESTION: What can I do to make the lender believe my financial statements are correct?

CONSIDERATIONS: Most lenders prefer to have an independent opinion on the reasonableness of the financial statements. You can have your accountant audit or review your financial statements and then issue an opinion on them.

QUESTION: What does it cost to incorporate?

CONSIDERATIONS: The cost of incorporation varies according to the complexity of the organization and the amount of professional help obtained. If you choose to incorporate yourself by buying a how-to manual, the cost will probably not exceed $100. On the other hand, if you go through a respected legal firm who advises you, completes the forms, and develops minutes for your meetings, and so forth, you can expect to pay approximately $1,000. If you elect to engage a legal firm as your corporate counsel on a retainer basis, you will probably pay between $200 and $500 per year for that service.

CHAPTER 3

Setting Up the Books

THE result of dreaming, planning, and working for your business is the bottom-line result reflected in the company's books.

The term "books" comes from the traditional use of bound journals and ledgers in which to record the financial records of a business. The books don't create the story: their purpose is merely to make available to those interested a record of the financial aspects of a business.

Maintaining financial records for the business is both a requirement of taxing agencies and a sound management principle. Without good financial records a business won't know whether it is losing or making money.

There is no one right way to establish and maintain financial records, just as there is no one right way to advertise a product. Different record-keeping systems will produce different financial statements. The right method of maintaining financial records is the way that is most beneficial to your business.

The options for implementing a record-keeping system are many, such as maintaining the records on paper or computer; using your accountant or employees to record the results of operations;

and switching revenue and expenses between different accounting periods. This chapter discusses the many considerations you must evaluate before setting up your books.

WHY KEEP BOOKS?

One of my first jobs as an accountant was to prepare the financial statements and tax records of a small restaurant. I was trained in the school of theory but not of practice. I understood the reasons for an organization's financial books, and also what they were supposed to contain. But I was rather surprised when I asked the owner for the financial records and he presented me with twelve unopened bank statements. "Is that all there is?" I queried, only to receive the answer I didn't want to hear: "Yep!"

This taught me something I had not been taught in school:

Only accountants like record keeping. Entrepreneurs don't get the same pleasure from establishing books and recording figures as accountants do. Entrepreneurs view the task as an unwelcome necessity.

People don't keep records of information they don't want or know how to use. Much of the data recorded for financial purposes is mysterious to many business people. As long as the bank was cashing his checks, my small restaurant owner saw no reason to maintain financial records.

Only accountants can establish adequate financial records. To the accountant, the need for records in business appears intuitively obvious and simple. Just as you wouldn't expect the average business person to design effective advertisements or create good blueprints to construct a building, you shouldn't expect to know how to establish financial records.

Accountants frequently establish record-keeping systems that are too elaborate for their clients. If you give a three-year-old child a hammer, it will find that everything in the house needs pounding. If you let your accountant establish the most exclusive possible set of records for your business, you probably are recording and collecting too much information.

You need to set up books in your business to meet the following three record-keeping objectives:

Record and present your financial condition. You need sufficient financial information to run your business effectively and profitably. (*Note*: You must tell your accountant what information you truly need if he is to set up any books to reflect that information. It is, in short, a participatory procedure.)

Provide sufficient evidence to support transactions. You need financial records to support the property of your assets, liabilities, net worth, income, and revenue to governmental taxing authorities.

Conform to generally accepted accounting principles (GAAP). Your record keeping must conform to generally accepted accounting principles so that it is comparable to that of other businesses and acceptable to banks and other regulatory agencies as a reasonable record of the financial status of your business.

WHAT TYPE OF BOOKS DO I NEED?

There are hundreds of books on accounting and accounting records, but few get down to the basics. They attempt to teach accounting, preparation of financial statements, and the fine art of speaking "accountese." All of this is of minimal interest to the entrepreneur.

For a moment let's throw away the books on accounting theory, generally accepted accounting principles, and financial-analysis methodologies and talk about what is really needed.

A basic set of books for any business should include these five items:

- *Checkbook.* The checkbook is the basic record for most small businesses. In fact, properly constructed it may be the only financial record a small business needs to maintain.
- *Cash-receipts journal.* In this book you record all revenue received and where it came from. If your customers buy from you on credit you can record the customer's name and then at the end of the month transcribe the amounts owed you to a "statement" you then send to your customer. (See Figure 1 for an example of a cash-receipts journal.)
- *Cash-disbursements journal.* In this book you record where you have spent your money. Obviously, both this and the cash-receipts journal are a duplication of some of the material in your checkbook. The reason you use a journal is to divide the disbursements into categories. (See Figure 2 for an example of a cash-disbursements journal.)
- *Payroll register.* Because of the taxes and other deductions withheld from employees, it is normally advantageous to maintain special records for payroll purposes. They also provide you with the type of summary you need to prepare annual year-end tax statements for your employees. In many instances this summary can be accomplished using your cash-disbursements journal.
- *Ledger.* The ledger is used at the end of the accounting period to prepare financial statements. The information included in your journals is transcribed to the ledger. All of the information on your financial statements, including not only revenue and expenses, but also loans, assets, and ownership equity, are entered in the ledger.

The checkbook is the simplest item for record keeping, and the ledger the most complex. Many businesses maintain their own checkbook, journals, and payroll records. Then, at the end of an

Figure 1

Cash-Receipts Journal

			Source					
Date	Customer	Amount	Sales	Tax	Freight	Bank Interest	Other	Specify Source
3/17	J. Jones	$110.00	$105.00	$4.20	.80			
3/19	Savings Bank					$8.76		
3/20	B. Smith						$50.00	Sale of scrap

Figure 2

Cash-Disbursement Journal

Date	Payee	Amount	Inventory	Rent	Purpose Office Supplies	Equipment Maint.	Other	Specify Purpose
3/15	Martin Management Co.	$580.00		$580.00				
3/17	Peters Co.	$385.00	$385.00					
3/25	Window Cleaners	$15.00					$15.00	Clean windows

accounting period, they have their accountant "close the books." The closing process includes transcribing information from the journal to the ledger and then preparing the financial statements. Generally it takes a basic knowledge of accounting to execute the closing process, but keeping the records needed for that purpose need not be that complex.

WHAT DO THE BOOKS LOOK LIKE?

Books come in all sizes, shapes, and colors, from simple to complex, manual to automated, inexpensive to expensive.

The more common types of record-keeping media are described below:

Bound journals/ledgers. Preprinted books available in most office-supply stores, for recording financial transactions. Some of these books leave space for you to write in the column headings, while others, such as cash-receipts journals, already include many of the more common captions.

Payroll registers. Preprinted registers for listing employees, their salaries, and all payroll deductions. Some payroll registers have one section for the calculation of gross pay and another for the gross-to-net calculation.

Spread sheets. Preprinted forms, usually sold in pads, for itemizing receipts or disbursements in the appropriate accounts. These spread sheets range from a minimum of two columns to fifteen or more columns in length. This could be considered a poor man's journal.

Pegboards. This method of recording usually combines the checkbook and the journal. Items are posted to the correct account at the time the check is prepared.

Point-of-sale registers. Sophisticated cash registers that can both record sales and make the distribution of sales to the proper accounts. Point-of-sale registers are sophisticated cash-receipts journals.

Financial forms. Worksheets to be completed by clerical

people that provide the necessary accounting information. Most franchises provide their franchisees with the necessary forms to record the results of their transactions. Generally, stores provide their cash-register clerks with forms that let them "check out" their cash receipts at the end of their shifts.

Automated bookkeeping systems. Small businesses can purchase computers complete with bookkeeping software systems that record information, usually via a terminal, and produce most of the needed financial statements. Using computers, nonaccountants can produce simple financial statements without having to acquire accounting skills.

Bookkeeping services. These services provide their clients with forms to complete that substitute for journals and ledgers. The forms are submitted to the bookkeeping service, which uses the information to produce financial statements.

Ask your accountant to assist you in selecting the media that are appropriate for your business. Your system should be reviewed at least annually.

STEPS TO ESTABLISH A SET OF BOOKS

Below are the steps for an entrepreneur to follow in establishing a set of books with his accountant.

Establish your financial-information requirements. The primary purpose of business books is to provide information to the entrepreneur. The books should be designed to provide that information.

Establish chart of accounts (ledgers). The chart of accounts indicates the kinds of accounting information that will be collected. The larger the chart of accounts, the more complex the record-keeping system. For example, you could have one account for all office equipment, or you could have numerous accounts: one for typewriters, one for copy machines, and so on.

Select points for recording information. The type of records maintained will be dependent upon where that information is collected. For example, if the information is collected at the point of sale, then the entrepreneur may want to select point-of-sale equipment to record financial transactions. On the other hand, if a marketing force is in the field it may be advisable to have that group complete forms, which can then be used as a basis for financial records. Or, if transactions are few and infrequent, simple spread sheets may suffice.

Divide accounting tasks between the business and the accountant. Those tasks to be performed by the business and those by the accountant should be defined. The entrepreneur should concentrate on how the tasks to be performed by the business are executed. He should also carefully review all work done by the accountant, since the company is ultimately responsible.

Make employees accountable. The people who do the recording should be accountable for their actions. Employees feel much more responsibility to do a good job when they know they are accountable. Accountability can be achieved by assigning sole responsibility to one person or by placing an employee's name on a document. Employees should be instructed how to perform the necessary tasks. In smaller organizations instruction can be oral, but in large organizations instructions should be formalized in written procedures.

Define methods of collecting information, the media for record keeping, and the process. Develop the procedures, methods, media, and the processes for actually doing the record keeping.

CONSIDERATIONS IN SETTING UP BOOKS

In establishing books for your business, you and your accountant should consider:

- *Costs.* The cost to establish your books should be consistent with the size of the business and the value of the

financial information to the operation of the business.
- *Financial analysis required.* The use of the information should be defined prior to collecting it.
- *Time.* How long it takes to complete the recording of the financial transaction.
- *Duplication.* The better systems record transactions only once.
- *Assistance to accountant.* If your accountant does part of your financial record keeping, those parts the business does should be designed to optimize your accountant's time. There should be little overlap of functions. Note that it is normally cheaper for the business to do the manual clerical functions than to have the accountant perform them.
- *Simplicity of operation.* The easiest way to do the record keeping is normally the best way.
- *Ease of retrieval.* Records are used to substantiate and support your financial transactions. The accounting system should make retrieving such supporting evidence easy. For example, if one of your customers questions his statement you should be able to retrieve his ledger, invoices, cash receipts, and debit or credit memos quickly and economically.
- *Satisfy legal requirements.* Your record-keeping system should be in compliance with accounting and statutory requirements.

Even in its simple form, record keeping is a costly and time-consuming part of your business. Don't overlook your accountant's contribution to developing and improving your system.

CHAPTER HIGHLIGHT

You can't make any money keeping records, but you can lose financial control of your business by not keeping records.

COST CONSIDERATIONS OF RECORD KEEPING

If you are concerned about the cost of record keeping ask your accountant these questions:

QUESTION: How much should I spend to establish a set of books?
CONSIDERATIONS: Generalized accounting records suffice for most businesses. You just need to be sure that the system will handle any special industry needs. Establishing a system should not take longer than one or two days of an accountant's time and perhaps two or three days of your time. Thus, for a business of under five people the cost should not exceed $200, and for most businesses it should not exceed $1,000. If you choose to automate your record keeping the cost and effort will be greater (see Chapter 7).
QUESTION: When should I consider getting automated equipment to do record keeping?
CONSIDERATIONS: At a minimum you should acquire a good ten-key adding machine at a cost of approximately $100. After that, you should continually analyze the cost of record keeping. A good rule of thumb is to automate whenever a recording task requires the equivalent of one person to spend one day a week recording transactions *or* there is a strong concern for control and accuracy. For example if you feel your employees may be stealing cash receipts you may wish to install a cash register to limit potential losses. See Chapter 7 for information on automated systems.

QUESTION: How much should I spend on maintaining a set of books?

CONSIDERATIONS: Two factors will significantly influence the cost: the amount of detail required and how closely the recording of financial information can be integrated into normal processing. The cost of keeping business books—including recording transactions, posting to the books, paying bills, and balancing books to verify that the transactions are properly recorded—should not exceed 2 percent of your revenue (plus the cost of your accountant).

QUESTION: Is it cheaper for the business to maintain the books or for an accountant to do it?

CONSIDERATIONS: The cheapest method is normally one that divides the tasks between the business's staff and the accountant. As a rule, the business should record all of the transactions, and the accountant should close the books. Larger organizations, which can afford to keep a professional accountant on staff, can close their own books.

QUESTION: How much do record-keeping supplies cost?

CONSIDERATIONS: The supplies needed for recording financial information normally only cost pennies a day, even when preprinted forms are used. Pegboard systems, which include checks, cost more than preprinted journals and ledgers, but the costs are still nominal. When people are replaced by machines, however, the cost of the equipment can be substantial. This is discussed in Chapter 7.

FINANCIAL INFORMATION CONSIDERATIONS

The questions you should ask your accountant regarding needed financial information include:

QUESTION: What types of financial information should I collect for my business?

CONSIDERATIONS: The types of information most businesses need for proper analysis of their business performance identifies sources of revenue, purpose of expenditures, profitability or nonprofitability of operations, and sources and uses of cash, and timing of cash flow. These basic requirements should be adapted to reflect the specific requirements of your line of business and requirements for financial information for the day-to-day operation of your business.

QUESTION: What types of records do I need for a budgetary system?

CONSIDERATIONS: The budget system is in addition to the regular accounting system but is based on approximately the same accounts. For each revenue and expenditure account you should have a budget. The budgetary statements are used to compare and monitor discrepancies between actual revenues and expenditures and the originally budgeted amounts.

QUESTION: When I establish my set of books should I opt for more or less information than I think I will need?

CONSIDERATIONS: Generally, opt for the minimum necessary information when you establish your books. After you have derived some financial statements and analyzed them, you will be in a much better position to determine what additional information—if any—you need.

HOW TO ASSIST YOUR ACCOUNTANT

The questions you should ask to optimize your accountant's time include:

QUESTION: What type of record keeping can I do better or more economically than my accountant?

CONSIDERATIONS: As a rule, accounting information can be gathered more effectively and economically by the business. Most of this information is collected in the normal course of work.

QUESTION: What do accountants want businesses to do to make their work easier?

CONSIDERATIONS: Asking your accountant's advice on the type of information to collect may be the single most valuable step you can take in making the accountant's life easier. Other steps that help him relate to neatness, accuracy, and completeness of the work presented to him. For example, it's a waste of an accountant's time when checks are recorded improperly, or when accounting entries are not explained, are difficult to read and interpret, or are consolidated when the accountant needs detailed information.

QUESTION: How often does your accountant need to be involved in closing and analyzing your records?

CONSIDERATIONS: Usually it is sufficient to interface with your accountant quarterly. The type of information you need for day-to-day activities should be readily available from the records maintained by the business. A quarterly review by your accountant should coincide with budgetary reviews (if you prepare budgets) and revisions of plans. More frequent review is normally unnecessary.

QUESTION: Should I reconcile bank statements, accumulate journal totals, and perform other end-of-month functions, or should I leave that to my accountant?

CONSIDERATIONS: You should undertake all of those tasks you can do easily and effectively. Leave for your accountant only those functions you do not understand or are uncertain about.

QUESTION: If I do more of the accounting tasks, should the accounting fee be less?

CONSIDERATIONS: Generally, yes, if you do it correctly, but this is something you should discuss in detail with your accountant. Knowing how much each service costs may help you decide who should perform what function. Keep in mind that if you do it wrong it will usually cost more to have your accountant correct your work than it would cost to have him do it initially.

CONSIDERATIONS OF SIMPLICITY

To make your accounting work easier, the questions you should ask your accountant include:

QUESTION: How can I simplify my accounting operation?

CONSIDERATIONS: Automation is the eventual answer for most businesses, but until it becomes economical to automate all or part of your accounting operations, you should attempt to perform as many operations concurrently as possible. For example, with pegboard accounting systems you record the check and post the transaction to the journal at the same time. This eliminates one step and thus simplifies the operation while saving time—and therefore money.

QUESTION: Is it simpler to record the transaction at the time it occurs or to do it in the evening after the business is closed?

CONSIDERATIONS: If you record transactions as they occur, there will be fewer errors. In addition, transactions should be recorded on a document that does not need to be transcribed to another document. The elimination of double recording reduces the cost, simplifies the system, and eliminates many errors.

QUESTION: If I buy an accounting system, such as a pegboard system, will it be simpler than one I develop myself?

CONSIDERATIONS: Any preprinted, well-defined system usually is simpler in form than a vague, generalized system. The advantage of a predesigned accounting system is that step-by-step instructions are given for using it correctly. This simplifies the recording task because people forget oral instructions and mistakes result . A predesigned system also simplifies utilizing temporary help to cover vacations and illness since the temps are more likely to be familiar with a commonly used system.

QUESTION: Do I have to balance my records to the penny?

CONSIDERATIONS: Very few organizations attempt 100 percent accuracy in record keeping. The argument for balancing to the penny is that there may be many large errors in opposite directions that net down to a small difference. This argument is usually invalid, however, and the cost of balancing should not be more than the amount of the difference. For example, if you differ by $1 from the bank statement, it is better to write off that dollar than to spend $5 trying to find the problem.

RETRIEVAL CONSIDERATIONS

To be sure you can retrieve the needed information from your accounting system, you might want to ask your accountant the following questions:

QUESTION: What type of evidence do I need to support my accounting system?
CONSIDERATIONS: Think in terms of what information you would need if you were taken into court and charged with making an invalid transaction. For example, if a customer stated that he had not received an order, you might want a signed receiving document to verify that the transaction was valid. The more common evidence that you should save includes:

- Invoices.
- Shipping documents.
- Checks.
- Receiving documents.
- Contracts.
- Tax-deposit receipts.
- Tax returns.
- Letters containing financial terms.
- Bank statements.

QUESTION: What documents will I want to retrieve most frequently?
CONSIDERATIONS: Those that enable you to answer questions about customer purchases, i.e. original invoices sent to you and orders you placed with vendors.
QUESTION: How should I store my source documents for ready retrieval?
CONSIDERATIONS: The method and frequency of retrieval usually determine the method of storage. Many businesses have found it helpful to store documents in more than one sequence by using a multipart form. For example, customer invoices can

be stored by date of purchase and customer name. Thus, if you know the customer name you can readily retrieve the document, or if you know the date of an order it can likewise be retrieved quickly.

Short-term storage is normally required for documents needed to answer customer or vendor questions and claims. Thus they should be stored either by customer/vendor name or date. A second copy of invoices, purchase orders, and shipping and receiving documents is helpful if many inquiries are expected.

Long-term storage is required for legal and tax purposes. The primary storage sequence is by tax year, and the secondary storage sequence is by account, such as payroll or inventory, so that you can support the balances on your tax returns. It is recommended that after your income tax returns are prepared you put all the supporting data in a single box (boxes for larger organizations) and mark the contents on the box, then store it in a secure location.

LEGAL REQUIREMENTS

Questions you should ask your accountant to ensure you are in compliance with legal requirements include:

QUESTION: How long must I retain accounting records?
CONSIDERATIONS: Legal requirements normally mandate seven years prior to the current calendar year and tax requirements three full years. It may not be necessary to save all records for that length of time. To reduce the cost of maintenance, determine the retention period for each type of accounting record and develop procedures to destroy that information when the period expires.
QUESTION: What is an audit trail, and how does that affect my business?
CONSIDERATIONS: An audit trail is a capability to reconstruct fi-

nancial processing. The audit trail requirements of the Internal Revenue Service require that you be able to trace source documents to the control totals in which they are accumulated and, conversely, to substantiate control totals by being able to trace them to all the source documents that comprise the control total. Even as an individual taxpayer you must maintain this audit trail or be liable for tax assessment for the inability to substantiate your personal financial statements.

QUESTION: Who from the government might examine my financial records?

CONSIDERATIONS: Probably a tax agent. There are many types of tax agents, including those examining business income tax, sales tax, and taxes paid on the value of your plant, equipment, and inventory. The agents will be from the federal, state, or local agency requiring the tax return. For example, Internal Revenue Service agents audit tax returns filed with the IRS.

QUESTION: Must my records be able to substantiate every penny of income and expenses?

CONSIDERATIONS: Technically, yes; practically, no. Revenue agents are generally reasonable if your records are in good condition. An occasional missing document would not be considered unusual.

QUESTION: Is one type of bookkeeping system better for legal purposes than another?

CONSIDERATIONS: The best bookkeeping system is the one that fulfills *your* legal and business needs. Legal requirements generally relate to the type of evidence you must retain, the adequacy of your audit trail, and the period of document retention.

QUESTION: If source documents such as invoices are unavailable because they are not needed for my business, can I still substantiate my revenue for tax purposes?

CONSIDERATIONS: Businesses need some method for proving revenues and expenditures. If you don't have invoices and other source documents, you should maintain a cash-receipts and cash-disbursements journal that contains such information as your customer's name and the type of service provided. Get a receipt for every business expenditure.

Now that you have a basic understanding of the many options available to you in relation to setting up your books, sit down with your accountant and discuss the specifics of your business and your likes and dislikes, so the two of you can develop the books that meet your needs.

Section II
BUSINESS PLANNING

Planning is important—remember, it wasn't raining when Noah built the ark.

CHAPTER 4
Financing the Business

MUCH has been written about the virtues of operating on other people's money; concepts such as "leveraging" explain how to make money that way. Yet in spite of all the disadvantages of financing one's business on one's own funds there is one overriding inducement to do so: you have complete control over the business when you exclude creditor involvement from it. Few businesses are cash-rich, either at the time they organize or throughout their lives. The need for cash is a continual concern.

Few business people understand the ins and outs of raising capital for their business. The tendency of many is to "tough it out." The prospects of raising and being responsible for other people's money may appear to be a poorer alternative than struggling to survive without the capital. Sometimes business people don't think they can borrow funds and thus don't try.

Financing your business and cash flow are two distinct problems. The latter is concerned with receiving revenue in time to pay one's bills; the former is the process of borrowing or otherwise raising capital. This chapter discusses the financing process and explains how your accountant can help with the decisions and processes of raising capital.

SO WHAT IF YOU DON'T HAVE ENOUGH MONEY!

Most of us know businesses that continually struggle to survive. They have a good product, the owners are competent, and yet they seem always to teeter a day or two away from bankruptcy. For these businesses, an infusion of capital may mean the difference between success and failure.

Let's examine the effects of insufficient capital on a business and then look at the uses to which additional capital may be put. The decision to raise venture capital, or to borrow funds, is a serious one requiring an in-depth analysis of the business.

The major impediment in an underfinanced business is the handicap underfinancing places on the mental attitude of the owner. The owner of a barely surviving business is reluctant to gamble its few available funds to capitalize on opportunities. Many businessmen feel that if they can just survive for a few more months things will get better. One is reminded of the old saying, "Cheer up, things could be worse, so I cheered up, and sure enough, things got worse."

For most businesses, "luck" is *made*. Those able to take advantage of an opportunity can expand; those who must either shortcut quality or pass up opportunity will probably continue to struggle forever.

Sufficient funds provide managerial independence difficult to obtain by any other means. People are much more willing to gamble one dollar when they have ten in their pocket than they are to gamble one when they only have one. In the first case, they have nine more chances to win; in the second, it is an all-or-nothing gamble. Few businesses are willing to play for stakes that high.

We need to examine the difficulties of underfinancing. The use of capital, when a business is organizing or during its life, explains both the positive and negative aspects of adequate financing.

The following represent the major uses of capital in a business:

- *Purchase of capital items.* Most businesses need property, plant, or equipment to perform their work. The office with high-quality furniture, decoration, and office equipment looks much more successful and professional than the office skimping by on much cheaper items. While a good-looking place of business doesn't guarantee success, studies show it is a factor in success.
- *Expansion into new areas.* When the brass ring is available, you should grab it. Most opportunities require money up front; without it you may have to watch someone else grab the ring and reap the rewards.
- *Adequate inventory.* Products are the lifeblood of an organization. Those that skimp on inventory may see their customers drift away. One large catalog showroom printed a beautiful brochure, but when customers came into the store they were frequently told the pictured product was out of stock. Many customers did not want to wait ten days or two weeks for the product to come in and began going to another showroom that had the needed product on hand. Eventually the constant shortages of inventory forced the original showroom out of business.
- *Purchase at quantity discounts.* Price breaks on quantity purchases may be significant. Having funds available to buy in large quantities and take advantage of discounts may more than offset the interest costs on borrowed funds.
- *Freeing of the owner's time.* Many owners are saddled with routine tasks such as bookkeeping, opening and closing the business, ordering and arranging products, and so forth because funds are insufficient to hire personnel to do these jobs. As a result, the owner may not be doing the tasks most beneficial to the business. For example, the owner might make

far more money selling the business's products than keeping the business's financial records.

On the negative side, some of the benefits of adequate capital can be offset by the constraints and strings attached to raising and retaining capital. For example when you borrow money you may be required to put up assets as collateral and you will not be able to sell those assets until the loan has been repaid. Before exploring capital considerations in depth, however, let's evaluate some of the alternatives to raising needed capital.

SOURCES OF FUNDS

Businesses use both traditional and unconventional methods for raising money. One is tempted to think of the bank as the primary source of funding, but it is only one of many such sources. Let's look at the ingenuity of business people in their quest for funding:

Bank loans. The granddaddy of all the ways of getting money, it is effective if your credit rating is good enough. Even the largest corporations go to the banks regularly to borrow money. The selection of a bank for your business accounts should be based on the bank's willingness to issue you a line of credit and to lend you funds. It is always a good idea to "take a banker to lunch" so that you have a friend in your local bank.

Personal funds. Many business people use their own funds and collateral for establishing their business. If more money is needed, more personal funds can be put into the business. Consider holding some or all such funds in reserve in case of an emergency.

Friends or business associates. If your business idea is so great, some of your friends or colleagues may wish to contribute to it, whether through loans at a specified interest, loans with options to buy stock later at a specified price, or loans that will result in a share of the profits during its term.

Venture capital. Many investors are looking to buy into

promising businesses. These investors are willing to risk capital but not their time in the venture. In most cases they do not want controlling interest of the business but are looking at the investment strictly from a profit perspective. If you sell stock for capital, you may want to retain the right to buy it back later at a specified price. Often your accountant will be able to inform you of potential investors.

Hold another job. Many people establishing a business need to work at another job during the formative years of their new business. Some businesses, such as selling, small manufacturing, or writing can be operated part time. In other instances, an entrepreneur may be able to hire people to run the new firm while he works at another job to ensure his own and the new business's financial security.

Customer financing. There are numerous ways to obtain business financing from customers. One small market-research organization required up-front money so it could run a job using the customer's funds. Other businesses offer their customers discounts if they will pay prior to receiving the ordered product. In the mail-order business, for example, you can take orders and use the money received to manufacture the product. Thus, the business does not require any major capital investment to produce its wares.

Vendor financing. Consignment is a popular way for vendors to introduce their products into your business. You pay nothing until you have sold the goods, at which time you remit funds back to the vendor. In some instances, the vendor will even give you promotional material and, perhaps, advertise its product in your area, either cooperatively with you or independently.

Tenant financing. Suppose you need an office or store for your business. To finance this you build a building much larger than you actually require. You obtain advances and rental agreements from tenants for the extra space; the deposit money is used to buy the building, and the rental income pays for the upkeep of the property. In effect, you acquire a rent-free office, since your tenants pay for your space. In return you are now a landlord and have commensurate responsibilities.

These are not the only ways to raise capital, but they should provide some insight into the range of options available to businesses. Normally the only limitation on raising capital is your own imagination and salesmanship.

CAPITAL CONSIDERATIONS

To borrow or not to borrow, that is the question. Answering requires an in-depth analysis of the individual business situation. The following should be considered in making decisions on raising capital:

Lost opportunity. Business opportunity has to be the main consideration for borrowing. The business person should evaluate the results of borrowing or not borrowing funds. If the cost of borrowing equals the profit to be gained from borrowing, then the net result may be a lot of work for the owner with no immediate profit potential. Businesses continually have opportunities to expand and to generate more profit. In many instances borrowing funds is the only means to take advantage of these business opportunities. Without careful analysis of the full cost of the opportunity, however, including borrowing costs, you may acquire an unprofitable opportunity. Before borrowing you should prepare:

1. a cash flow statement for the business opportunity.
2. an estimated statement of income and expenses.
3. a plan to staff and manage the new opportunity.

Cost of raising and repaying capital. Raising capital entails two expenses: the cost of obtaining money (some methods of borrowing involve high interest rates); and the cost of amortizing interest and principal on funds borrowed. The amount of these expenses affects not only the choice of whether to borrow or not but the means of obtaining money. For example, a short-term unsecured loan may be prohibitively expensive, but a long-term second mortgage may be an acceptable expense.

Strings attached. Nothing is free. When people give you money, they expect something in return. Before taking a loan, find out what happens if you miss a payment or two. Before you sell stock, investigate your loss of control of the business and evaluate your obligations when customers, vendors, or tenants finance your business.

Tax considerations. The cost of borrowing is tax deductible for the business. Therefore, depending on your tax rate, the government may end up paying a substantial part of your cost of raising funds. In some tax districts interest-free loans are made as a means of attracting business to that area. Some local municipalities provide special tax breaks for companies locating in their area, and these breaks may more than offset the cost of borrowing to relocate or expand.

One of your friends in this decision-making process is your accountant. He will be familiar with bankers and investors whom you may not know. Not only can your accountant help you decide whether or not to borrow, he may be the one who makes borrowing possible.

QUESTIONS ABOUT OPPORTUNITY

Questions you may wish to ask your accountant regarding business opportunities include:

QUESTION: If I were to increase the amount of capital available to my business, would I thus create opportunities to increase my business's revenues or decrease expenditures?
CONSIDERATIONS: Accountants work in many businesses and industries and gain insights into potential revenue opportunities, or methods for reducing expenditures. Much of this knowledge is through management consulting. Most accountants prepare an annual letter to client management suggesting areas requiring attention, but usually not in enough detail so

that you can implement the suggestions without some assistance. Nevertheless, some general, probing questions can provide you with insight into areas of potential gain. A few good suggestions from your accountant may more than offset the cost of all your accounting expenses.

QUESTION: In reviewing my books and analyzing my accounting records, does the accountant see areas of waste or mismanagement that could be eliminated if my business had greater financial resources?

CONSIDERATIONS: Many expense problems in a business, such as not taking advantage of price discounts when you buy products in large quantities, can be corrected only by a greater infusion of capital into the business. The accountant may feel it is not worth mentioning these areas to you because in analyzing your financial statements he knows you cannot afford to remedy the situation. In addition, your accountant may not mention these situations because he does not have the specific facts, and it is not the accountant's primary job to look for areas where you can reduce your expenditures. But if the accountant knows that extra funds may be available, an additional list of recommendations should be made.

THE COST OF RAISING AND REPAYING CAPITAL

Questions you should ask your accountant about the cost of debt are:

QUESTION: Am I paying too much for my debt services?

CONSIDERATIONS: Many businesses take on debt in a piecemeal fashion. Sometimes the costs of many small debts are larger than necessary, and the accountant, recognizing the situation, may be able to offer alternate funding sources that can reduce the cost of debt. There are many ways to calculate interest, so even the interest rate quoted can be misleading. Simple interest is the cheapest method for calculating interest, in that you pay the amount of interest quoted on the unpaid balance. Interest that is deducted from the balance borrowed and compounded interest will cost you more money than the same percent of interest charged as simple interest. In addition, there may be service charges to place the loan and premiums for life insurance required by the lending organization. (The insurance is on you with the organization as the beneficiary.)

QUESTION: How do I determine how much debt is too much?

CONSIDERATIONS: Accountants use industry ratios to measure the amount of your debt. The most common debt ratios are:

1. amount of debt to owners contribution to the business.
2. amount of debt to amount of assets.
3. amount of interest to amount of revenue.

QUESTION: Do I have too much debt for my business?

CONSIDERATIONS: The previously stated debt ratios provide guidelines on the amount of debt a business should incur. A realistic amount of debt varies by industry, your rate of growth, and profitability. The accountant can analyze your financial statements and provide you with some guidance on how much debt is realistic for your line of business and current economic condition.

QUESTION: Is the interest I am paying on my debt realistic in today's market conditions?

CONSIDERATIONS: You can ask your banker or investment counselor what debt costs and whether that is reasonable, but the accountant knows what organizations are paying for their debt and can tell you whether your percentage of interest is realistic, relative to other businesses of your type and size. If the interest is too high, you may wish to consider alternate methods of debt.

QUESTION: Is my business eligible for government-backed low-interest loans?

CONSIDERATIONS: Many governmental districts provide low-cost loans to businesses for a variety of reasons. The United States Small Business Association provides such loans, while many tax districts provide a variety of tax breaks for organizations relocating in their area or doing business in certain industries. Accountants, through their contacts with government agencies and other clients, may be aware of sources of low-cost loans for your business. (See Appendix A for a listing of government agencies that help small businesses.)

QUESTION: Am I taking maximum advantage of interest deductions for tax purposes?

CONSIDERATIONS: The loan payment dates and sometimes the method of calculation of interest affect the deduction that can be taken in the current business fiscal year. When constructing a loan, ask your accountant's advice to ensure that you maximize this interest deduction.

"STRINGS" CONSIDERATIONS

To minimize the impact of debt on your business, you should ask your accountant the following questions:

QUESTION: What penalties do I face if I am forced to miss one or more debt payments?

CONSIDERATIONS: Newspapers continually carry stories of people able to pick up a $25,000 property for a few hundred dollars' payment of delinquent or unpaid back taxes. Most bankruptcies are triggered by the failure to pay debt at a specified time. Most lending agreements call for harsh penalties in the event your business fails to meet payments by a specified date; the business person should be aware of them and of how to avoid them.

QUESTION: If I am unable to meet my debt payments, are there procedures I should take to minimize the penalties?

CONSIDERATIONS: Businesses in financial trouble should immediately discuss those problems with their accountant and with their creditors. It may be particularly helpful to have your accountant call a creditor and explain the financial situation and the proposed solution. Most creditors prefer not to invoke penalties because they want repeat business from their customers and they lose revenue if their clients go bankrupt. If your accountant can convince the creditor that you have a temporary cash-flow problem or short-term business problem, he may be willing to develop a mutually acceptable alternative repayment plan.

QUESTION: Does use of low-cost business loans place any long-term restrictions on my business?

CONSIDERATIONS: There is no free lunch. When you get something that sounds too good to be true, it usually is. Government agencies provide low-cost loans because they want something. In some districts such loans require locating your business in that area for the life of the loan and maybe longer; in other instances they may require some government oversight of your business. Check the small print carefully.

QUESTION: Can my creditors gain control of my business?

CONSIDERATIONS: Some forms of raising capital, such as bonds and stocks, may grant certain rights to your creditors. Some of these conditions may not take effect until you fail to meet certain predetermined conditions, such as making payments on specified dates, while other forms of raising capital immediately delegate control to your debtors. Again, read the small print carefully.

TAX CONSIDERATIONS

Tax planning is an important part of capital formation and should receive careful scrutiny.

QUESTION: What happens to investment tax credits and interest-payment tax deductions if my business is not making a profit?

CONSIDERATIONS: Most tax benefits are applied to reducing taxes owed on profits. If your business is unprofitable, you may be able to apply tax advantages to either previous or future years' profits. Your accountant can advise you on how to maximize the tax benefits of debt.

QUESTION: If my business cannot take advantage of tax benefits, are there ways I can personally benefit from those deductions?

CONSIDERATIONS: Many entrepreneurs whose businesses are losing money but who are personally making money shift ownership of depreciable assets to themselves. In other words, you buy the asset as an individual and then rent it to the corporation. You can then personally take the investment tax credit and deduct the interest payments, even if the business can't do so. There are, however, some tax rules about renting to your business and about the amount of rental you should charge the business. Your accountant can advise you on this.

QUESTION: If the business has extra funds, can I as an owner borrow from the business at minimal or no interest?

CONSIDERATIONS: It is a common practice for owners to borrow from their businesses. Most owners repay those loans before the end of the business fiscal year, because the Internal Revenue Service may challenge you on the basis that long-term loans are really dividends and are therefore taxable.

QUESTION: Should I expand my business during profitable times so I can benefit from the tax write-off of interest payments?

CONSIDERATIONS: You may, when profits are high, have a tendency to borrow and expand the business because interest is tax deductible and so it appears that the government will be paying a substantial part of the interest. Bear in mind that the primary purpose of borrowing funds should be to improve your business or your competitive position in the marketplace. While there is an advantage to having the government subsidize your borrowing through tax credits, this should not be the main reason for borrowing. On the other hand, if tax deductions for interest and investment tax credits make the business more profitable or competitive than it otherwise would be, that should be utilized to advantage.

QUESTION: If my debt payments become too large for my business, what can I do to reduce them?

CONSIDERATIONS: The most common method for reducing debt payment is to refinance short-term debts with a longer-term loan. This will increase the total amount of interest but reduce the monthly payment. Another method of decreasing debt payment is to sell stock to raise capital to pay off the debt. This method may be difficult for organizations with a high ratio of debts to assets, because potential investors may be reluctant to invest in a business with extensive debt.

CHAPTER 5
Establishing Plans and Objectives

PETER decides to embark on a trip and in preparation purchases a very expensive power yacht fully equipped with radar, radio, life preservers, and other necessities for an ocean voyage. In order to buy the yacht, Peter has mortgaged his home, borrowed heavily, and worked hard for a number of years learning yachting. He is now ready to begin. With great fanfare he departs. There is plenty of activity as the ship cruises from the safe waters of the harbor into the turbulence of the ocean. "Where to, captain?" yells the first mate. Peter responds, "Full speed ahead—let's move." The first mate keeps asking the ship's heading, and the captain keeps responding, "I'm too busy running the ship to chart the course, just keep going full speed ahead."

Storms appear on the horizon, and the ship is battered by large waves and begins to take on water. The first mate yells, "We're taking on water, what should we do?", but the owner is too busy running the ship to spend the time and energy to bail out the boat. "We're sinking, captain!" yells the first mate, but the owner keeps responding, "Full speed ahead." Eventually, the inevitable happens and the ship sinks. The captain can't understand it. Everybody worked so hard, all to no avail.

Many businesses, bedecked in their finest regalia, begin with the same fanfare but within two years have sunk into the murky waters of insolvency. Many owners, like the captain of the fine yacht, are confused and disappointed at the "bad luck" they have encountered.

Most bad luck is man-made. Many businesses fail to chart their course when they begin. Then, as the business begins to founder, they neither recognize the problem nor want to take the appropriate action to correct it. The owners are too busy working to plan.

Lack of adequate planning is probably the primary reason for business failure. Other reasons are stated, but I suspect they are the symptoms of inadequate planning.

Planning is painful, time-consuming, and does not appear to affect profits directly. But the ultimate rewards of good planning are high profits, acceptance in the business community, survival, and other characteristics of success that sometimes seem so elusive.

THE PLANNING CYCLE

Planning is not a single event but, rather, a continuous process. People who plan build planning into the everyday activities of their business. Those who do not plan regularly probably view it as an annual activity.

Planning is a managerial function that should be performed by the owners or senior officers of the corporation. This does not imply that other individuals are excluded from the process but, rather, that they provide input to the process as opposed to doing the planning itself. Planning should drive the business, rather than the reverse. It should be not a confirmation of current activities but the establishment of future direction and activities.

Good planning does not ensure success, but it certainly helps. Of course we are all familiar with many of the great planning feats of history that resulted in disaster. Howard Hughes spent millions of dollars to build the Flying Goose. This huge wooden aircraft never flew a combat mission. The Ford Motor Company spent millions of dollars planning, designing, and producing the Edsel. It was not the right product for the time and was withdrawn from production. Both Howard Hughes and the Ford Motor Company did extensive planning, and yet their projects were not successes in the marketplace.

On the other hand, there are millions of planning successes. Unfortunately, we seem to remember the failures more than the successes. Almost all major corporations grew through intensive planning efforts.

HOW BIG DO YOU HAVE TO BE TO PLAN?

The small business may have to do more planning than the large one in order to succeed, but, the small business may not need the same resources or scope in planning as the larger one. The results of planning are important, not the methods.

One corporation, a small manufacturing plant, was able successfully to compete with a giant in the industry. The planning of the corporation was not nearly as extensive as that of its giant competitor, but it was equally effective. When asked about their marketing policy, the small-business people responded that they obtained the price lists of the big corporation and then priced their own products 10 percent lower. That was their marketing strategy plan. The company recognized that the giant corporation had spent thousands of dollars studying the market, estimating the cost of the products, and then developing a price that would provide them with a fair profit. The small business knew that without the layers of middle management necessary for the giant to succeed it could successfully underprice by 10 percent and still make a reasonable profit. And it did. The planning was quick but effective.

The small-business person will probably do most of his planning individually. In addition, the accountant can provide valuable input into the process. Accountants understand planning and can provide the manager with financial information about the business necessary for planning purposes.

Let's examine how a small business might determine its marketing plan for the next twelve months. The basis for the plan is provided by the marketing objectives, which specify the product line the business will handle, and its marketing method. The objectives set the planning parameters.

The planners would then begin to look at marketing opportunities and constraints. For example, availability of product is a constraint. The business cannot sell more product than it can make or obtain. Other constraints, such as size of the market, acceptance of the products by the marketplace, and funds available for manufacture and marketing all help shape the marketing plan. The planners must make estimates on who will buy their product or service and the quantity customers might purchase. Plans should not be based on wild guesses but on well-thought-through, realistic objectives. The plan must include a rational approach to selling and distributing the marketing quotas set.

At the conclusion of the planning process, the business should know:

- Quotas for sales by product.
- Target customers by product.
- Advertising/promotion plans.
- Marketing quotas by salesperson, or direct-mail promotion.
- Methods to obtain needed services or product.
- Area to store products.
- Capability to service customers.

PLANNING CONSIDERATIONS

Planning is a never-ending cycle, as illustrated in Figure 3. It commences by setting business objectives that require plans in order to be accomplished. Feedback data is needed during the implementation process in order to analyze, adjust, and effectively integrate the plans into changing business conditions. As new conditions are recognized, new objectives need to be established— and the planning cycle continues.

Figure 3
PLANNING CYCLE

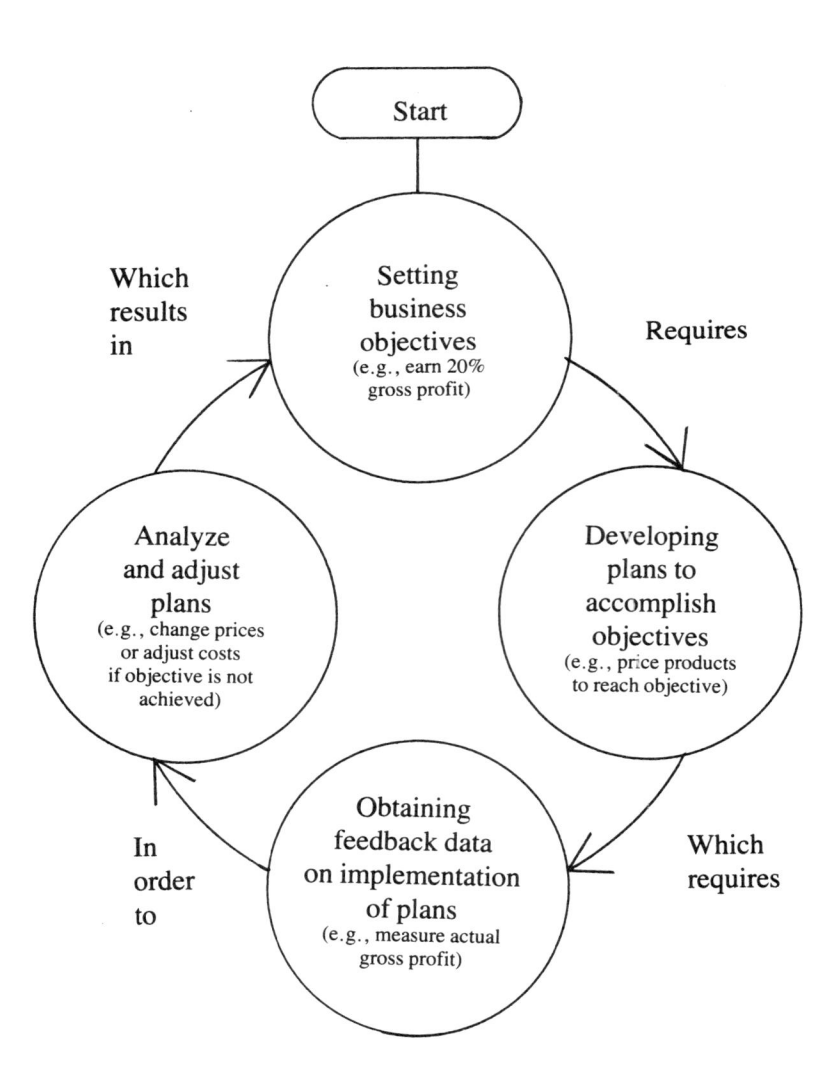

Start

Setting business objectives
(e.g., earn 20% gross profit)

Requires

Developing plans to accomplish objectives
(e.g., price products to reach objective)

Which requires

Obtaining feedback data on implementation of plans
(e.g., measure actual gross profit)

In order to

Analyze and adjust plans
(e.g., change prices or adjust costs if objective is not achieved)

Which results in

The planning cycle outlines the areas of activity that must occur if planning is to be successful. While setting objectives is important, alone it does not ensure success. Achieving that elusive goal normally requires going through all four parts of the cycle.

Setting Objectives

Unsuccessful businesses wait for things to happen. Successful businesses make things happen. There are three types of businesses: those that make things happen, those that watch things happen, and those that don't know what's happening. Setting objectives makes things happen.

What does it mean to set an objective? An objective is an event that you would like to have happen in or to your business. You decide for your business what events you want to occur.

Let's assume your business is producing a product—a piece of art, a food product, or a garment. In order to develop the products needed for your next business year, you should set some production objectives or goals. These objectives might be:

1. Reduce the cost of making the product by 5 percent.
2. Increase production capacity by 25 percent.
3. Reduce the defective products produced to less than 1 percent of production.

Obviously there are a lot of factors involved in achieving these objectives, but without setting some *measurable* objectives there are no goals to achieve. Without some direction employees aren't sure what is expected from them—in other words what constitutes a good job or poor job. A word of caution: setting goals too high has a negative effect on workers once they realize the goals are unattainable.

Develop Plans

Plans are the means of accomplishing objectives. They are the blueprints to follow to accomplish stated objectives. Without plans, the objectives may never be achieved.

Let's examine the objective of reducing costs of production by 5 percent. Planning must decide how best to accomplish that objective. Some alternatives that could be considered include developing a more effective way to make the product, buying raw material more cheaply, and substituting lower-cost materials for higher-priced raw material. Once the method has been selected the detailed plan can be prepared for achieving the stated objective.

Feedback Information

Feedback information is an analysis of the accomplishment of plans. It provides the basis for determining whether or not implemented plans are effective. In your home, a thermometer tells you the temperature. If your objective is to keep your home at sixty-eight degrees and your plan is to have a heating unit and air-conditioning unit to accomplish that objective, then your thermometer is the feedback instrument, or monitoring device, that tells you whether or not your plan is successful.

Feedback mechanisms are devices, reports, or analyses that monitor the status plans. For example, if the marketing staff is provided sales quotas, feedback information indicates actual sales versus sales quotas. The feedback mechanism, in this example the accounting system, collects data on sales and includes that data in a report. Without this type of information the owners will not know if their objectives are met.

Analysis/Adjustment

The last phase of the planning cycle is to measure the accomplishment of the plan, using feedback information. If the plan is not being achieved, action must be taken. If the temperature in your room is eighty, your feedback mechanism tells you to make an adjustment to your air-conditioning unit to lower the temperature to meet your objective. The same process occurs to your business plan. Feedback information is of little value until it can be compared against objectives. A combination of objectives, plans, and feedback information enables you to analyze the status of your plans. Business plans likewise can be adjusted if sufficient feedback information is produced and analyzed.

QUESTIONS ON SETTING OBJECTIVES

If you need help in establishing objectives for your business, you may wish to ask your accountant the following questions:

QUESTION: Is there information available about my industry to help me establish objectives for my business?
CONSIDERATIONS: Many accountants prepare or have access to industry reports and statistics. Most of the larger CPA firms prepare reports for their audit staff so they will have a general familiarity with particular industries. This type of information, describing the industry's characteristics and trends can provide valuable comparative input for setting your own business objectives.
QUESTION: Can you prepare special financial reports about my business that will be helpful in setting objectives?
CONSIDERATIONS: Your accountant prepares a predetermined set of financial statements for you. These may be valuable in analyzing your current operations, but may not be overly helpful for setting objectives. For example, a special trend analysis showing the sales pattern of particular products over time may tell you where to put your selling emphasis in the future. Your accountant may have some excellent ideas on the type of information that would be helpful in setting objectives

but he has not volunteered this information because you have never asked.

QUESTION: Should the objectives for my business be reviewed for their reasonableness by an independent source?

CONSIDERATIONS: Only the owners of the business can establish its objectives; that is not the accountant's function. Your accountant can, however, make an independent assessment of those objectives and tell you if they are consistent with the objectives of other similar businesses in your industry and are within your financial ability to accomplish. If they are not within your current financial scope, your accountant may have recommendations about how to obtain the needed capital to finance your venture in order to meet the objectives.

QUESTIONS ABOUT PLANNING

If you are uncertain as to how to proceed with planning, or what effective planning tools and techniques are, you may wish to ask your accountant:

QUESTION: What documents should I include in my business plan?

CONSIDERATIONS: Four documents that should be part of any effective work plan are a budget, a schedule, a work program, and a cash-flow statement. A budget indicates the business's estimated revenue and expected expenditures; a schedule indicates when the events in the budget will happen (e.g., the volume of sales by month); a work program outlines what is to be accomplished and who will perform specific functions to achieve the objectives; and a cash-flow statement shows your ability to fund your operation.

QUESTION: How formal do these planning documents need to be?

CONSIDERATIONS: The formality of the documents is unimportant. They can be prepared in pencil or on the back of an envelope. They should be as formal as the business warrants. A small business should not devote an extensive amount of time to preparing formal planning documents. Some rough, penciled notes for a business with two or three people may be sufficient, while larger organizations may desire more formal planning documents. Regardless of the degree of formality, the plan should state what is to be accomplished in measurable terms, when it is to be accomplished, who is responsible for accomplishing specific items, and the resources allocated for executing the plan.

QUESTION: How long a time span should the plan cover?

CONSIDERATIONS: Most corporations work with an annual plan, but new businesses may find it advantageous to work with shorter plans, perhaps three to six months. Furthermore, new businesses may not yet have enough insight into twelve-month periods to make realistic plans of that duration.

QUESTION: How much detail should I include in a budget?

CONSIDERATIONS: The object of a budget is to set some goals and constraints. The revenue part of the budget represents goals, the expenditure side constraints. The measurement of actual revenue and expenditure against budgeted amounts becomes the basis for changing plans. For example, if actual revenues are less than those budgeted, the business may need to make various adjustments to bolster sales or reduce expenditures.

QUESTION: What procedures should I follow to develop a budget for my business?

CONSIDERATIONS: Budgeting is an integral part of the planning process. It requires you, as owner, to think through the dollars associated with your detailed revenue and expenditure objectives. For example, if you intend to sell X products during the next twelve months, you must estimate the revenue from those sales. Then you must estimate the manufacturing cost of those sales, any commission that your sales staff will receive, the cost of shipping the product to the customer, and other direct costs of making a sale. Subtracting these costs from your revenues results in your gross profit. Next, calculate the cost of administering your business. This includes items such as rent, telephone, taxes, and electricity. These figures provide the equivalent of financial statements based upon the objectives you have set for your business. The difference between your budgeted revenues and expenditures is your anticipated profit for the budget period. If the profit is lower than you desire, you need to sell more, make adjustments in the selling price of your product, or cut the cost of obtaining or producing your product, or cut your overhead.

QUESTION: Can my accountant prepare a budget for me?

CONSIDERATIONS: The accountant can prepare the budget if you have established the basic objectives. The actual budget-preparation process is quite simple after the goals and objectives for the budget period have been set. If you have been in business for a period of time the accountant has most of the cost figures needed to prepare the budget. If not, he may well have comparative industry data. Of course, your accountant will charge you for this service.

QUESTION: What type of schedule and work plan should I prepare for my business?

CONSIDERATIONS: Again, the planning process is designed to direct daily work toward meeting your goals and objectives. Some types of business require very detailed schedules and work plans. For example, if you are in manufacturing you may have to order materials months ahead of time, hire and train people, and order or build equipment to produce the product. Without schedules to specify when all of these tasks must occur and a work plan showing who is responsible for what task, your production goals may never be achieved. Other businesses do not require such detailed planning.

QUESTIONS ABOUT FEEDBACK

If you are uncertain of the methods for providing feedback information to monitor plans, you should ask your accountant the following questions:

QUESTION: What procedures should I establish to provide feedback data?

CONSIDERATIONS: The accounting systems that collect financial information should also collect any needed feedback data. The work program can normally be monitored through either the inventory system or the revenue system. For example, if a business sells products, the current inventory provides the necessary feedback to monitor acquisitions or manufacturing; if the business deals in services, the revenue or contracts obtained in deliverance of those services similarly provides some feedback data.

QUESTION: What type of specific feedback information should my business collect?

CONSIDERATIONS: The business needs to collect feedback on the amount and sources of revenue, the products or services added or deleted from inventory (note that services can be recorded in terms of the addition or subtraction of people to the workforce), and administrative expenses.

QUESTION: How can I present feedback data so that it is readily understandable?

CONSIDERATIONS: Feedback data should be presented in special reports, such as a budget status report, schedule status report, or workload status report. A budget status report shows actual financial results compared to expected or budgeted results; a schedule status report shows actual accomplishments (such as filing a tax return on April 1) compared to the date scheduled (e.g., April 15) for that; and a workload status report shows work units performed versus expected work units, such as producing 580 products during January compared to a projected production of 550. Feedback data is always compared to the budgeted amount to show when and where variances occur.

QUESTION: How frequently should I prepare feedback reports?

CONSIDERATIONS: Monthly is normally adequate for a going business, but if there is a cash-flow problem, or the business is newly started, you may wish to monitor certain types of feedback information—such as the effective use of part-time people—more frequently. The main criterion in determining frequency of monitoring is how quickly owners are willing to take action on information they receive.

ANALYSIS AND ADJUSTMENT QUESTIONS

Questions on analyzing and making adjustments to planning information include:

QUESTION: Can accountants provide an analysis for the execution of business plans?

CONSIDERATIONS: The accounting system collects much more than pure financial data. For example, point-of-sale registers can record products sold, who sold the product, and the category of sale. Your accountant can accumulate and represent this information in a variety of formats. It's important for you to explain to your accountant the type of analytical information you need and how much it is worth to you to collect it. You may find that needed information can be collected as a byproduct of another accounting operation and adds practically nothing to the cost of accounting.

QUESTION: Can the accountant propose adjustments on the basis of the planning analysis?

CONSIDERATIONS: There are many areas in which the accountant is well qualified to recommend adjustments: on the amount of inventory maintained, economical order quantities for buying products, and other financially related adjustments. Adjustments that pertain to adding or deleting products or expanding or contracting areas of business are normally managerial, not accounting, decisions. The rule of thumb is to solicit accounting advice on accounting matters, and managerial advice from managers.

QUESTION: Couldn't I make analyses and adjustments based on actual business conditions without spending time and effort to set objectives, develop plans, and collect feedback information?

CONSIDERATIONS: You can, but is it more effective to use business intuition or scientific business methods? Some entrepreneurs have been very successful running their businesses on intuition, but the failure rate of the large majority of new businesses appears to indicate that most managers do not make good intuitive judgments. Bad decisions are less likely to be made when all the facts are known, and the objective of the planning cycle is to provide just those facts.

Section III

BUSINESS OPERATIONS

A plan is only a plan until it is put into operation.

CHAPTER 6
Living with Taxes

THE only exciting reading about income taxes consists of stories on how to avoid paying them. Preparation of the tax return is a sad time for most businesses, as they see the fruits of their labor forwarded to the government. The harder you work and the more money you make, the more the government takes.

The amount of income taxes paid, and, therefore, the bottom-line profit on your statement of income and expense, can be legally changed. With planning, and within limits, your business can determine how much tax it will pay in a given year. Tax planning is an important part of business planning.

The tax laws are highly complex and it is difficult at best for an individual, and even one accountant, to understand them. In addition, small, closely held corporations should consider the combined effect of the tax on the business and the owners' personal income taxes.

Many businesses engage an accountant primarily for tax advice. Get your money's worth: a good tax accountant can probably save you more than you will pay him for his service.

EVASION VERSUS AVOIDANCE

There are two methods to reduce the amount of taxes you pay to the government: one is legal, the other is not. Both, however, may bring you into a confrontation with the federal, state, or local revenue service.

Tax evasion is illegal and should be avoided. "Evasion" means that you purposefully fail to report revenue or claim more expenditures than you actually incurred. For instance, some businesses pocket cash receipts and do not report them as income. These and other practices are subject to both criminal and civil penalties.

On the other hand, tax avoidance is legal and encouraged by most accountants. Avoiding taxes is accomplished by delaying payment into another tax year and by reducing the amount of tax due. Tax avoidance is accomplished by taking advantage of all the provisions in the tax laws that are beneficial to you. As a general rule, most accountants advise businesses to take the maximum deductions allowed. This will enable them to "avoid" as much tax as possible. When taking maximum deductions, the business should be prepared to be challenged by the appropriate revenue service. Many such deductions are questionable, and the tax courts may not have fully decided on the legality of specific deductions.

Tax avoidance can either reduce or delay your taxes. For example, the investment tax credit on the purchase of assets is a credit provided by the government to encourage such purchases. Taking the credit actually reduces your taxes. On the other hand, accelerated depreciation of your assets may benefit your tax situation in the short term but only delay the payment of taxes in the long term: you will be using assets for years when you can no longer claim any depreciation, since you have already used up the allowable depreciation. No deductions will be allowed in those future years.

Taking questionable deductions to avoid taxes is not a violation of the law. For example the difference between a casualty loss (a quick loss due, for example, to damage or theft), which is deductible, and termite damage, which is not deductible, is clear, but there is a gray area in between the two extremes where deductibility is not clear. If the revenue service rules a deduction invalid, it will charge you the additional taxes, and interest on those taxes, if the filing date has passed—but there will be no criminal or civil penalties due to tax avoidance.

COMPLETING TAX RETURNS

One of life's unhappy tasks is spending hours filling out forms to assess your income taxes. Depending upon the area in which your business is located, you may be paying income taxes to local municipalities, state or provincial government, and the federal government. Each has different forms, all requiring time and effort to complete.

The starting point for preparation of an income-tax return is your financial statements. The records you keep for tax purposes may well be different from those used in the preparation of your business financial statements. It is not necessary that the two be identical, but some tax returns request an explanation of differences between them. For example, you may use straight-line depreciation for your business statements while using accelerated depreciation for tax purposes.

The steps you should follow in preparing income-tax returns are:

- *Step 1: Identify taxing districts.* Identify all of the districts in which you must pay taxes and then obtain the appropriate returns and instructions for completing those returns.
- *Step 2: Gather financial information.* When preparing to complete the returns you should gather copies of your business's financial statements, last year's tax

returns, and identify any differences between your financial statements and your tax statements.
- *Step 3: Transcribe your financial information to the tax return.* Following the instructions, compute your tax base or taxable income.
- *Step 4: Calculate the tax and identify tax credits.* Use the tax tables to calculate your tax. Your business may be eligible for many tax credits, such as the investment tax credit or the new-jobs tax credit. The calculation of tax should not be considered complete until you have reduced the calculated tax by all appropriate credits.

TAX ESTIMATION AND PAYMENT

If you thought preparing a return was hard, making a tax payment may be even harder. One is knowing, the other is paying. However, there are some options available in paying business income tax.

Corporations, like individuals, are normally required to prepay an estimate of their annual tax bill. Federal returns call for the quarterly payment of estimated tax, while state and municipal income taxes may have different schedules. While the time of payment is fixed, the business has some leeway in the amount of tax paid.

As a general rule, your estimate for the current year is based upon taxes actually paid the preceding year. Normally, if a business pays as much estimated taxes this year as they paid the previous year in actual taxes, there will be no penalties, even though actual taxes are significantly higher than estimated taxes.

Businesses should plan to pay the minimum estimated taxes. Funds not submitted to the federal government can be invested and earn interest for the business rather than the government. Timing the payment of estimated taxes is another integral part of tax planning for the business.

Businesses should also do quarterly tax planning. The statement of income and expense at the end of each quarter will provide a basis for estimating taxes. It also gives the business enough time to make adjustments during the remaining quarters of the tax year in order to modify the amount of tax owed at the end of the year prior to closing the accounting records. The two major tax-planning sessions should be at the beginning and end of the year. At the beginning, the major tax-planning decisions should be made; at the end, adjustments can be determined.

TAX RECORDS

Businesses are normally required to retain tax records for three full calendar years in addition to the current year. At the end of the three years it is generally safe to destroy the records. To be safe, however, businesses should consult with both their accountant and legal counsel before doing so. Unfortunately, the three-year rule does not apply to all tax records. For example, the records supporting the purchase of capital assets need to be retained three full years past the last year in which depreciation was taken for that asset. If the asset has a ten-year life, the records would then be retained for thirteen years. The same retention rules apply to other long-term assets and debts.

The types of records that need to be retained for tax purposes include:

- Funds contributed by owners/stockholders.
- Records supporting the purchase of capital assets.
- Loan agreements.
- Invoices, contracts, and so on supporting the revenue shown on the tax return.
- Bills of sale, receipts, and so on supporting the expenditure of funds.
- Travel and entertainment explanations. Normally receipts for travel and entertainment expenditures by them-

selves are insufficient for tax deductions. The business must show the purpose of the expenditure, the people visited, and the participants in meals and entertainment expenses in order to substantiate the bill as a legitimate business expense.
- Recreational-vehicle substantiation. If your business uses automobiles, airplanes, boats, and so on that may jointly serve as recreational vehicles, it is normally required to maintain a log of usage to substantiate the business use of that vehicle.
- Employment records. Substantiation that funds paid to individuals was in return for services rendered.

BUSINESSES AS A TAX SHELTER

A tax shelter is a legal method open to anyone of hiding or sheltering income from the tax collector. It is a legal way of avoiding paying taxes. Tax sheltering normally takes advantage of a special provision of the income-tax laws. The business itself can be a tax shelter, or the business can include a tax shelter. Some of the more sophisticated tax shelters permit you to save more in taxes than you invest in the business.

Let's look at two tax-shelter examples:

A business as a tax shelter. A major tax shelter for businesses is real estate. People can establish a business to make money in real estate while sheltering their profits from the tax collector. Let's assume a business is buying and selling homes. Assume that it buys a $100,000 home for 10 percent down and a 90 percent mortgage at 10 percent interest. It rents the home to an individual for $1,000 a month, creating a revenue of $12,000 per year. Further assume that it pays $1,000 per year in real-estate taxes and we can depreciate the home over twenty years (i.e., 5 percent depreciation per year).

Now, let's examine the tax sheltering of the $12,000 income.

	Tax Profit/Loss	*Cash Flow*
Income from rental	$12,000	$12,000
Less 10% interest on $90,000 mortgage	−9,000	−9,000
Less property taxes	−1,000	−1,000
Less depreciation of 5% of $100,000	−5,000	
Total loss on business	$−3,000	$ 2,000

The net result of the tax shelter is that the individual received the use of $2,000 extra cash tax free. This results from subtracting the out-of-pocket costs, the interest on the mortgage, and the taxes, or a total of $10,000 from the $12,000 income. In addition, the individual has a $3,000 tax loss to apply against other income. If the individual is in the 50 percent tax bracket, that $3,000 tax loss will result in a tax saving of $1,500.

The net result of the tax shelter is that the individual receives the equivalent of $3,500 cash on a $10,000 investment, or a 35 percent return on investment after taxes. It would require a pretax income of $7,000 to generate the same amount of cash. In other words, the individual has made the equivalent of a pretax return on investment of 70 percent—a phenomenal rate for someone who might put his money in a savings bank at 5 percent interest. Yet tax shelters of this magnitude are easy to establish and operate.

Business tax shelter. Funds earned in the business can be sheltered from taxes. One of the most common methods is through use of a pension plan. Family-operated businesses, with sufficient planning, are able to shelter all of their earnings from taxes if they so desire.

Let's look at a personal-service business. Assume the individual has an outside income from investments or other businesses and desires to shelter all of the income generated from the personal-service business. Assume further that the business has a corporate structure.

The owner of the business establishes a "defined-benefit" pension program. In other words, the business defines the amount of retirement income it will pay its employees per month. The company is now allowed to deduct whatever funds are needed to provide the defined-retirement benefit. If the individual starts the business at age fifty and plans to retire at age sixty with a significant monthly income, the premium to fund the defined benefit can be huge. The business contracts with an insurance company to provide the defined benefit and then pays the premium out of its profit. It is possible to have larger tax deductions than the revenue generated by the business.

TAX CONSIDERATIONS

Income taxes may consume a large percentage of your profit. The tax rate is too important to leave to the tax collector. You and your accountant should take the steps necessary to minimize your business income taxes. The criteria you should consider in determining your tax are:

- *Tax planning.* The strategic and tactical planning required to take advantage of the provisions in the tax laws that will reduce your tax payments.
- *Tax preparation.* The methods and procedures to prepare and submit the return to the taxing agency.
- *Tax payments.* The forwarding of the tax funds due the taxing agency.

CHAPTER HIGHLIGHT

Tax planning is an important aspect of all business decisions. That you should pay unnecessary taxes is not the intent of the government nor is it in your own best interest.

TAX-PLANNING QUESTIONS

In the development of tax-planning strategies, ask:

QUESTION: Should my business use the calendar year as its tax year?
CONSIDERATIONS: There are two major advantages to having a different tax year than calendar year: receiving salary and bonuses at a more personally advantageous time from the tax viewpoint; and obtaining accounting services at reduced rates because it is not the accountant's busy time of year.
QUESTION: Is my business entitled to an investment tax credit?
CONSIDERATIONS: When you purchase capital items, your business is generally entitled to investment tax credits in the year in which it purchases the capital items.
QUESTION: How do I get the maximum investment tax credit?
CONSIDERATIONS: The percentage of investment tax credit is normally related to the length of time over which the asset is depreciated. Currently in the United States the maximum investment tax credit is 10 percent. To obtain the maximum investment tax credit you may have to depreciate the asset over the life prescribed by the Internal Revenue Service, currently seven years.
QUESTION: Are there other tax credits for which my business is eligible?
CONSIDERATIONS: Taxing authorities normally offer businesses a variety of tax credits. Changes in the business laws affect the type and amount of such credits. Businesses should continually query their accountants about those available so they can take advantage of the tax credits to which they are entitled or change their business plans to maximize the credits for which they are eligible. Examples include tax credits for creating a new job (thus it may be advantageous to add more employees than to pay the existing employees overtime); for conserving energy; rehabilitating old buildings; employing handicapped; and conserving natural resources.

QUESTION: Who should be involved in tax planning?
CONSIDERATIONS: Tax planning is the responsibility of the business. Accountants and lawyers are consultants to the business in doing that planning. Employees responsible for taxes should collaborate with consultants who provide input into tax-planning strategy.

QUESTION: When should tax planning occur?
CONSIDERATIONS: Tax planning is an annual event in which you develop your tax strategy for the coming year, so it should best be done just prior to the beginning of your fiscal year. The plan should then be reviewed at least quarterly, when financial statements are prepared. The statements will indicate whether or not income projections are in accordance with tax projections. If not, adjustments can be made.

QUESTION: How can I shelter my income from the tax collector?
CONSIDERATIONS: Tax laws provide a number of different ways to shelter income—many of which are risky. For example, if you invest in oil exploration and fail to hit oil you will lose your funds. Other tax shelters are to buy existing real estate, make movies, build buildings, and lease equipment; all are subject to some risk. Therefore, your tax planning must establish a strategy for your business. If the strategy is to shelter all income, there are some excellent methods of accomplishing this, primarily through pension plans. On the other hand, if your objective is to provide a livelihood for yourself and to expand the scope of your business, your tax planning may involve a different strategy, such as a store-purchase plan, buying more assets for your business, or establishing benefit plans, such as 100 percent medical coverage that lets the business pay expenses you previously have been paying personally.

QUESTION: How can I reduce my taxes without taking risks or losing control of my cash reserves?
CONSIDERATIONS: There are numerous methods available to businesses to reduce their annual tax rates. Four hypothetical methods might be:

- Using accelerated depreciation.
- Increasing bad-debt write-off.
- Prepayment of expendable supplies and tools.
- Prepayment of employee bonuses.

In addition, there are other methods for reducing the amount of taxes, many industry-oriented, such as the depletion allowance provided for the petroleum industry. Discuss these industry-specific methods with your accountant.

QUESTION: Can I use my business to reduce my personal expenses?

CONSIDERATIONS: Businesses can provide individuals with personal benefits paid for out of business tax dollars. For example, in another chapter we discuss a corporate medical plan that reimbursed employees for 100 percent of their medical expenditures above those paid for by the firm's hospitalization plan. Let's assume that the individual is in the 50 percent tax bracket and does not have enough medical expenses to qualify for personal medical tax deductions. If that employee should incur $1,000 of medical expenses in a year, that individual would need to earn $2,000 in order to pay for the medical expenses. The additional $1,000 is needed to pay the tax on the $2,000 income so that $1,000 will be available to cover the medical expenses. If the business reimburses the individual, it can do so with pretax dollars, so it will only cost $1,000 for the business to pay $1,000 of medical expenses. Other business-reimbursed or partially business-reimbursed personal expenses include:

- Taking vacations in conjunction with business trips.
- Buying your automobile for the business. (NOTE: you must deduct the percentage of time or mileage it is used for personal matters.)
- Hiring your family and paying them a salary to buy their own personal items. (NOTE: you need to substantiate what they did.)

QUESTION: Can I legally shift some of my home and furnishing expenses to my business in order to gain the advantage of paying those expenses with pretax dollars?

CONSIDERATIONS: Two major tax advantages are available to the owner of a business. If the business is conducted in the owner's personal residence, that part of the residence used for the business is tax deductible. Generally, whatever area is used for the business should be used exclusively for the business. This permits the business to deduct depreciation and a percentage of home-operating expenses. In addition, all of the equipment and furniture in the business area is fully deductible by the business. The owner can also purchase an automobile and use it partly for business, partly for personal transportation deducting that percentage of the automotive charges that relate to business purposes.

QUESTION: Suppose my business is losing money—do I still get the personal benefit of the tax deductions?

CONSIDERATIONS: If your business is a sole proprietorship or a subchapter S corporation you can deduct the loss from other personal income. If your business is a corporation, you do not get the advantage of the loss offset against your personal return.

QUESTION: If I do not expect my business to make money during the developmental stages, how can I take advantage of investment tax credits and the tax-saving uses of business losses?

CONSIDERATIONS: Gaining these deductions shows the importance of tax planning. Assuming you expect to lose money, or break even, during the first few years, and you incorporate (not as a subchapter S corporation), then you lose your business's current investment tax credits and the benefits of a business loss. These losses can be applied against future corporate income but the credits may expire before you can use them. However, the business can require you as an employee to maintain your own equipment and place of business. You can charge depreciation, get investment tax credit, and deduct other expenses incurred individually against your own outside income. In other words, you can shift enough business expenses to your personal income so that the business operates at close to a break-even position. Generally, you can take any personal expense you incur, such as travel or supplies as a personal business expense on your individual tax return in lieu of charging your business for that expense.

QUESTION: Can I regulate through personal salary and bonuses the amount of money my corporation earns so I do not have to pay corporate income taxes?

CONSIDERATIONS: If you do not want your corporation to make money, you can pay yourself year-end bonuses that approximately equal the corporate profit as a means of avoiding paying both corporate income tax and personal taxes on the same funds.

QUESTION: If I perform personal services, is there a tax problem in leaving money in the corporation and paying the lower corporate tax rate, rather than taking the money as personal income at a higher tax rate?

CONSIDERATIONS: If the corporation is established as a personal holding company, you may be subject to very high personal holding-tax rates. If this is of concern, discuss it with your accountant and lawyer, since it is a highly complex area of taxation.

QUESTIONS ABOUT TAX PREPARATION

If you are concerned over the preparation of your returns, ask your accountant:

QUESTION: Do my tax returns have to be prepared by the tax-due date?

CONSIDERATIONS: Most taxing agencies will provide an extension. Normally, however, you have to file for that extension (even though it may be granted routinely) and pay your estimate of the proper tax by the filing-due date. If you underpay your tax, you may incur interest and a nondeductible penalty on the delinquent amount.

QUESTION: Must my tax return be typed?
CONSIDERATIONS: You can file your return in any manner you want, as long as it provides the appropriate information.
QUESTION: Am I better off having an accountant prepare my tax return?
CONSIDERATIONS: Having a tax expert prepare your return gives you several advantages. First, you get professional advice; second, the consultant signs the return, which indicates to the various revenue services that a qualified person has filed your return; and third, in the event your return is questioned, you can be represented by the individual who completed the return.
QUESTION: If my return is audited, should I go to a hearing, send my tax accountant, or should both of us go?
CONSIDERATIONS: Normally, it is better for your tax accountant and the revenue agent to discuss the issues without you present. First, you are emotionally involved; second, you may volunteer information that could damage your case; third, you may be asked questions about items other than those being audited. Your accountant knows tax auditors and can plead ignorance easier than you can. Let the accountant resolve the matter for you.

TAX PAYMENT QUESTIONS

If you have concerns about the timeliness of your tax payments, you should ask:

QUESTION: How do I estimate my income tax?
CONSIDERATIONS: Your estimated taxes can be based on last year's actual taxes or expected taxes based on your business budget. In general, if you expect to make more money this year than last year, you will still choose to pay estimated tax based on last year's taxes. This reduces the amount you have to pay during the year, thereby giving you longer use of your funds. But increase the amount of your last payment.

QUESTION: What happens if I underpay my estimated taxes?

CONSIDERATIONS: The result of underpayment of taxes can be interest on the unpaid balance, a penalty, or both. Some businesses, in periods of high interest rates, underpay their taxes because the interest charged by the government on delinquent taxes is less than the interest the business can earn by investing the amount of underpayment.

QUESTION: If the taxing agency assesses a higher tax for my business, should I pay the assessment or fight it?

CONSIDERATIONS: If you believe the figures on the tax return are proper, you should fight the additional assessment. If high penalties and interest are involved, you may choose to pay the amount initially, then fight the decision and request a refund. If the assessment is a result of an error made on your return, or you agree with the taxing agency's challenge, then you should pay the assessment. Businesses should not be intimidated by an audit or an additional assessment.

CHAPTER 7
Automating Systems

THE computer, it is said, has been the dominant creation of the twentieth century. The machine has made it possible to put a man on the moon and to snarl up your personal department-store charge account. Everybody has his own story about the use—and abuse—of computer systems.

To compute or not to compute, that is the question facing many businesses. The advertisements depicting the computer as a problem solver are enticing. On the other hand, there are enough problems related to the use of computers to justify concern.

The salaries of the people who can be replaced by automation are escalating, yet we read that computer technicians are in scarce supply, are more costly to hire than clerical people, and are difficult to supervise if a manager does not possess some data processing skills.

This chapter examines the computer, your accountant, and you. Many businesses look to their accountant for advice on when to computerize and then for help in obtaining, installing, and operating the computer.

DO I NEED A COMPUTER?

Most businesses can benefit from the services of a computer, so the real question is whether or not it is economical to install one. Very often the answer will be yes.

If your answer to one or more of the following questions is yes, you are a candidate for a computer:

- Do you have more than ten employees?
- Do you have over fifty customers that you invoice?
- Do you have over 100 items of inventory in stock?
- Do you write more than twenty-five checks per month?
- Does your financial record keeping take over two hours per week?
- Do you regularly schedule work for over ten people?
- Does it take you more than sixteen hours to consolidate the information you need for financial closings and/or tax returns?
- Do you work in the evenings on your financial record keeping?
- Are you contemplating adding staff for record-keeping functions?
- Does your record-keeping volume fluctuate significantly during the month or year?

Most businesses need a computer, but the thought of being responsible for one can be mind-boggling to many people. The time spent learning the computer should be paid back many times over through the elimination of tedious, time-consuming clerical tasks and through improved speed and accuracy of paperwork processing.

DEFINING COMPUTER TASKS

The first step in acquiring a computer is to define what tasks the computer will perform. Generally, the computer is more effective than people in performing high-volume, repetitive functions. Volume is partially related to the effort required to accomplish tasks and their repetitiveness. For example, a payroll of ten employees could warrant obtaining a computer, whereas providing for two employees might not.

The following two methods should be used as a basis for defining computer tasks:

Method 1: Time-consuming tasks. The clerical tasks performed in the business should be listed with the number of person-hours expended to perform those tasks. For example, payroll might require two hours per week, invoicing customers six hours per week, etc. Those repetitive tasks that consume more than one hour per week of people time should be considered candidates for automation.

Method 2: Business decisions. A list should be prepared of the repetitive decisions made in your business—such as when to order more inventory, whether to approve customer credit, and so forth. Estimate the number of such decisions made per month. If the result is more than ten per function per month, the job is a candidate for automation.

WHAT DOES A COMPUTER COST?

The cost of a computer comprises the following components:

- *Hardware (the computer).* The physical piece of machinery you buy.
- *Software (the systems).* The programs or applications you purchase or write in order to process data on the computer.
- *People.* Individuals you need to hire to develop systems, to prepare data, and to operate the computer.
- *Space.* The floor space set aside for the computer.

- *Supplies.* The printer, forms, tapes, disks, and such used in operating the computer.
- *Maintenance.* Tasks performed on the hardware and software to keep them operational.

The above list indicates that the cost of computer hardware is *not* the major expense of obtaining and using a computer; in most cases it is only a small part of the total. The cost of running a computer depends on the type obtained and its method of operation. Micro or mini computers with sufficient computing capabilities for some small businesses are available starting at approximately $1,000. But most small businesses would need a computer in the $5,000 to $12,000 price range, with supplies to get it started costing $1,000.

The major cost of a computer system will be for the application systems, or "software," as it is known in the trade. Most computer vendors offer software for their hardware, normally at additional cost. If your business can operate within the restrictions of prepackaged, purchased software, it is probably the most economical way to obtain programs since you aren't paying for custom programming. Most small ccomputers offer software in the following areas:

- General ledger.
- Sales analysis.
- Payroll.
- Inventory.
- Accounts payable.
- Accounts receivable.
- Statement preparation.

Software systems may be purchased for as little as $50 or as much as several thousand dollars.

Programmers, computer operators, and data entry operators may or may not be needed to run your system. Using the lower-cost alternative, you can purchase software and train yourself and your staff to operate the computer thus avoiding additional salaries. The higher-cost alternative involves adding computer personnel. Your choice will depend, obviously, on the complexity of your needs, the systems that can meet those needs, and your budget.

To Buy, to Lease, or to Use a Service Bureau

The alternatives you have for acquiring computer capability are:

- *Buy*. Purchase your own hardware and software.
- *Write*. Hire data processing professionals to develop customized software for your business.
- *Lease*. Lease hardware and/or software.
- *Service bureau*. Have an independent company provide you with computer services.

The decision on whether you buy or lease is dependent on the following factors:

- *Length of service desired*. The key decision is the expected length of time that the hardware or software will satisfy your needs.
- *Economic analysis*. On the basis of the number of years of useful life, the purchase price, the lease price, and the value of money, a mathematical analysis can be made to determine whether rental, purchase, or leasing is the most cost-effective solution.

The in-house-versus-service-bureau decision depends on your need for technical electronic data processing (EDP) skills. If the business's computer requirements cannot be satisfied with purchased software, the company will need some in-house people with data processing skills. Generally a small business is better off using the service bureau to develop systems than hiring and supervising data processing people. The service-center decision is not irrevocable. If the cost or volume of processing with a service bureau increases rapidly, the business can reconsider its decision and use the in-house alternative when it becomes more economical.

WHAT DOES THE OWNER NEED TO KNOW ABOUT THE COMPUTER?

The owner should know as much about the computer as he does about any other piece of automated equipment in the business. This knowledge is generally limited to the machine's capabilities and functions, that is, *what* it can do, as opposed to *how* the machine actually works. For example, an individual can use an automobile very effectively by knowing its capabilities and operating characteristics, but without knowing how the motor works or being able to repair the car.

The owner of a business should know the following about a computer, whether it is in-house or at a service bureau:

- *Processing capabilities*. The types of work that can and cannot be performed on the computer. If someone asks whether a particular task can be run on his computer, the owner should know.
- *Systems run on the computer*. The tasks or applications that are being run on the computer and the frequency with which they are run.
- *Operation of the system*. The owner should have enough knowledge about his system to operate the computer.
- *Interpretation of computer reports*. The owner should understand the types of reports produced by the system and the meaning of the information on those reports.
- *Service agreements*. The owner should know the responsibilities of the service to operate and maintain systems and the responsibilities of the vendor to keep its hardware and software operational.
- *Computer failures*. Both computer hardware and software

are subject to failure at any time. It is important, in operating a computer, to maintain sufficient data so that if the information being processed is destroyed through such a failure, that processing can be reconstructed and operations can continue. The owner must have an effective contingency plan before relying too heavily on computer processing.

COMPUTER CONSIDERATIONS

Automating a business with a computer is a major decision. Careful planning is the key. If the owners do not have sufficient data processing skills, planning should involve someone knowledgeable about the computer. Many accountants can fulfill this role.

The areas you should consider when evaluating whether or not to automate your office functions are:

- *Requirements*. The tasks you desire to automate.
- *Data processing skills*. Obtaining and keeping individuals with sufficient data processing skills to ensure success.
- *Hardware*. The physical computer.
- *Software*. The systems and programs that process data using the computer hardware.
- *Computer operations*. The day-to-day operation of the systems.
- *Backup and recovery*. Restoring computer operations after a problem occurs without losing critical data.

CHAPTER HIGHLIGHT

The acquisition of a computer should be based on both a need for the capability, and a commitment to expend the management resources necessary to make it work.

REQUIREMENT QUESTIONS

If you are uncertain about how to specify your requirements, you may wish to ask your accountant:

QUESTION: Does my business need a computer?
CONSIDERATIONS: The value of a computer is related to how much more economically or effectively tasks can be performed on it. If the job can be done cheaper and faster by the computer, or the computer can supply better information, then the business should obtain a computer.
QUESTION: What are my requirements?
CONSIDERATIONS: Your requirements are the output documents you want produced by the computer: invoices, paychecks, status of inventory reports, financial statements, and so on.
QUESTION: How should I specify my computer requirements?
CONSIDERATIONS: The requirements can be documented on plain paper in everyday English. They should be described in as much detail as practical. The key to the successful use of the computer is defining and documenting what you want done on it.
QUESTION: How do I know how long it will take to process my requirements on the computer?
CONSIDERATIONS: During the requirements phase, that is unimportant. What the owner should estimate is how long it takes

to perform the tasks manually. This will help determine which tasks should be computerized and in which sequence.

QUESTIONS ABOUT EDP SKILLS

If you are uncertain of the types of EDP skills your business should possess, you can ask your accountant:

QUESTION: What type of EDP skills should my staff and I possess to effectively utilize a computer?

CONSIDERATIONS: The skills are dependent upon whether application systems, such as payroll, are purchased or developed, and whether the computer is in-house or outside, that is, with a service bureau. The more you do to develop and run your own systems, the more skills you will need.

If a service bureau does the work, all your people need to know is how to prepare input for the computer application, how the application works, and how to interpret and use the results of processing. When the applications are executed in-house the level of skill needed increases. Computer operators must be hired or trained, and if problems occur, in-house personnel must be skilled in detecting and correcting the problem. The highest skill levels are needed if you develop and program your own applications. At that point you will need capable systems analysts and programmers. While your existing personnel can be trained to prepare and use computer data and operate the computer, it normally takes several years of experience to become proficient in computer-systems design and programming.

QUESTION: Where can I obtain needed EDP skills?

CONSIDERATIONS: Data processing personnel can be hired through want ads or through service groups such as accounting firms, employment agencies, or local data processing associations. If you want to train your own staff, contact your vendor for local schools that give classes in programming, repair, and so on.

QUESTION: How much will I have to pay to hire a computer programmer, data entry operator, or computer operator?
CONSIDERATIONS: The prevailing wage can be obtained by calling a local computer vendor, an employment agency, a business of equal size, or your accounting firm.
QUESTION: Can my accounting firm supply me with data processing expertise?
CONSIDERATIONS: Some accounting firms have accountants or other consultants knowledgeable in data processing, but not all firms possess these skills, nor the ability to lend their personnel to your company. They may also come into contact with people they can refer to you. It never hurts to ask.

HARDWARE QUESTIONS

In selecting hardware, you may want to ask your accountant the following questions:

QUESTION: What vendor should I select for hardware?
CONSIDERATIONS: The availability of vendor support, computer programmers, operators, and service groups depends on the quantity of a particular computer model in your area. It is usually sensible to go with the dominant computer vendor in your area.
QUESTION: Should I purchase or lease my computer?
CONSIDERATIONS: You should perform an economic evaluation to determine the most cost-effective solution for your business.
QUESTION: Can I negotiate price when buying a computer?
CONSIDERATIONS: Generally, the hardware price is nonnegotiable, but the services and vendor support are negotiable. In other words, you may be able to receive some computer programs and technical support as part of the deal when you purchase the hardware.
QUESTION: Should I buy my computer from the vendor who made it?
CONSIDERATIONS: There are many businesses that buy new com-

puters in quantity and then provide their customers with special beneficial financial arrangements. In addition, there is a good used-computer market, which will enable you to buy equipment at reduced rates. Usually, therefore, it makes sense to buy from a secondary source other than the manufacturer.

QUESTION: What hardware devices should I acquire?

CONSIDERATIONS: The size of the computer and what devices are attached to it will depend on your processing requirements. Both your accountant and computer vendor can help you determine the capacity required. Normally, you will need both a central processing unit (the CPU) module, a keyboard, a video-display screen, and a printer. In many cases, the first three elements are combined into one piece of hardware.

SOFTWARE QUESTIONS

If you are uncertain about the needed software, you can ask your accountant:

QUESTION: Should I purchase software or develop my own?

CONSIDERATIONS: The skill level required to purchase and use software is considerably less than that to develop software. It is usually far better to accept the restrictions of purchased software than to hire a staff and develop your own.

QUESTION: Where can I purchase software?

CONSIDERATIONS: Software for the more widely used computers is available from the computer vendor, independent software houses, other users of that particular computer (user groups), and accounting firms.

QUESTION: How can I determine what software is available?

CONSIDERATIONS: The computer vendor should be able to tell you what software is available for its equipment. In addition, there may be user groups that maintain an inventory of programs for the computer you select, some of which are available at no cost.

QUESTION: How can I learn to use purchased software?
CONSIDERATIONS: Some of the criteria for determining whether or not to buy a particular software package is the completeness of the user documentation, the simplicity of its operation, and the ease in which it can be understood. If you find you can't operate with the software, ask the seller to demonstrate its use or watch another company run its program.

QUESTION: How much will software cost?
CONSIDERATIONS: The cost of the software is determined by its complexity and the effort required to develop it, as well as by the size of the market for that software. Thus, specialized and highly technical software will normally cost more than general-purpose, easy-to-develop software. Prices of software packages vary significantly but generally are much lower than the cost of developing the package yourself.

QUESTION: Can I have changes made in the software?
CONSIDERATIONS: Most vendors will make changes in software packages to satisfy your specific needs, but they normally charge for it. In addition, if the vendor makes general improvements to the software, which is a common practice, you will need to have the new package changed again, which will add more to the cost of the vendor improvement, should you want it.

QUESTION: What do I do if my software stops working?
CONSIDERATIONS: If you are uncertain about the cause of the problem, you may want to rerun the system to determine whether the situation reoccurs, or you might want to eliminate the transaction that caused the difficulty. If this will not permit operations to continue, contact the vendor to identify and fix the problem.

QUESTION: How long does it take to fix software?
CONSIDERATIONS: Fixing software may take days or weeks. Because of this, restart procedures are attempted. The length of time to fix software is dependent upon the availability of the appropriate vendor personnel.

OPERATIONS QUESTIONS

If you have concerns over computer operations, you may wish to ask your accountant:

QUESTION: Should I hire a skilled operator to run my computer?
CONSIDERATIONS: With many small computers a person requires only a few hours of instruction to run the equipment. As computers get larger they become more complex; therefore it may be desirable to hire a skilled operator for such equipment.
QUESTION: How many operators should I have?
CONSIDERATIONS: It is important to have more than one person trained in the operation of a computer. As a general rule, two or more employees should be trained, in addition to one of the owners or managers.
QUESTION: How many hours a day will my computer be operating?
CONSIDERATIONS: Length of operating time depends on the size of the computer's workload. If it is used heavily for daytime functions, it may be in continuous operation. If it is used only for limited, discrete office operations, operating time may be negligible.
QUESTION: If I use a service bureau, how do I get my work run?
CONSIDERATIONS: Your agreement with the service bureau should specify the type of service to be provided and the time frame for completion of that work. Some service bureaus require you to bring the work to them, whereas others will pick up the work at your place of business.

BACKUP AND RECOVERY QUESTIONS

To make sure that your computer installation is adequately protected from problems, check with your accountant on the following:

QUESTION: Does a computer vendor supply me with backup and recovery procedures?

CONSIDERATIONS: The vendor may provide you with some software aids to help in the backup and recovery process, but it is usually up to the business to establish its own contingency plans.

QUESTION: What type of information will I need for the backup and recovery process?

CONSIDERATIONS: Backup and recovery requires that you retain sufficient information to reconstruct processing, should you lose all of the information in the computer. This probably will include computer files, copies of your programs, and transaction data.

QUESTION: Should I store some of my data off-site?

CONSIDERATIONS: As a general rule, protect your information by storing it away from the primary site. In many computers, this is easy since all you need do is save an old version of the file and your programs. You may want to keep the backup data at your home or possibly in a safe-deposit box. In the case of computers without removable discs you must keep input media, or occasionally print out the permanently stored data on paper and store it off-site.

QUESTION: How do I know whether my recovery process will work?

CONSIDERATIONS: Test the recovery process on a regular basis. Be sure to train your staff in the use of recovery procedures.

QUESTION: What can I do if the computer hardware is the cause of the problem?

CONSIDERATIONS: Many businesses make agreements with other users or the vendor of that hardware to provide backups in the event of problems. If the computer is relatively inexpensive, you may want to consider having two, in case one should fail.

CHAPTER 8
Pricing Your Product

A SMALL manufacturing company developed a product that was well received in the marketplace. Sales grew rapidly, and shortly that product was the company's best-selling product. In fact, they were having difficulty producing enough product to meet consumer demand. As sales continued to increase, the company began experiencing cash-flow problems. Even though customers were paying their bills on time, the company struggled to meet its payroll and pay its supply invoices. In desperation they engaged an accounting firm to help them solve their cash-flow problems. Unfortunately, cash flow was not the difficulty. The problem was that the company was selling its product for less than it cost them to make it. The more products they sold, the more they lost, until the cash-flow squeeze became tangible.

Many businesses are unable to develop realistic pricing policies often because of influence by competition or lack of sufficient accounting information to accumulate all of the costs needed to determine profitable selling prices. The objective of this chapter is to explain the methods used by businesses in calculating selling price, and then review pricing considerations.

CONCEPTS OF PROFIT

Two categories of profit are used by accountants, gross profit and net profit. Unless the two are clearly understood and differentiated, entrepreneurs can make serious pricing-strategy errors.

Net profit is the money made by the business. After all the revenue is tallied and all the expenses subtracted from that revenue, the result is called net profit. Even though there are a lot of accounting games played in deriving this amount, the figure is a reasonably good estimate of the profitability of the business. If net profit is positive, things are going well; if negative, you may be in serious financial trouble.

Gross profit is a profit based on the sale of your product. It represents how much money you made from selling a product over what you paid to make or buy the product. It ignores all of the administrative costs and thus is not a realistic estimate of your total net profit. It also is not a good indicator of the success of the business because it ignores many of the costs of doing business, such as invoicing customers; consequently it should not be used alone for pricing products. A gross profit based on sales can be misleading if you don't understand accounting.

It is easiest to explain gross profit by explaining what it does not include: management salaries; administrative costs, the salaries and benefits of the administrative staff; office equipment; postage; utilities; and taxes of all types. Generally, gross profit only includes those costs for the purchasing, manufacture, and sale of the product.

Figure 4.

Example of Profit Calculation

GROSS RECEIPTS OR SALES		$300,000
Less: cost of goods sold		
Inventory sold	$75,000	
Sales salaries	85,000	
Wrapping/shipping supplies	15,000	$175,000
GROSS PROFIT		$125,000
Less: administrative costs		
Advertising	$ 5,000	
Rent	40,000	
Telephone	1,000	
Office supplies	1,000	
Administrative salaries	15,000	
Depreciation	4,000	
Taxes	2,000	
Interest	1,000	
Repairs	1,000	$ 70,000
NET PROFIT		$55,000

Figure 4 is a typical calculation of gross profit and the items to be deducted in arriving at net profit.

PRODUCT-PRICING STRATEGIES

Pricing strategies are often complex and confusing to many businesses. The strategies are influenced by such trite phrases as "charge what the market will bear." However, this is but one of many pricing strategies that a business can use. Let's review the seven basic pricing strategies:

- What the market will bear.
- Fixed price.
- "WG" method ("Wild Guess").
- Competitive pricing.
- Purchase price plus overhead.
- Cost to produce plus.
- Desired percent of profit.

What-Market-Will-Bear Strategy

It is not necessary to have a direct relationship between cost and price. Businesses may be tempted to feel that if it costs one dollar to produce product X, it should be sold at a price within a reasonable range of the production cost. But, it is not uncommon for cosmetic manufacturers to price their products several hundred times the cost of manufacture. In fact, many times the inflated cost of a product is a status symbol. For example, consultants may charge $1,000 a day or more for their services. This is an indication of how valuable they think they are and may, in fact, make them more desirable than if they charged considerably less.

The disadvantage of this pricing strategy is that when your price is more than the market will bear it may be difficult to reduce the price. For example, if our $1,000-a-day consultant reduced the daily rate to $500, organizations may view it as an indication that the consultant is no longer desirable. The same can occur when any product price is reduced: Its prestige may be lost once the price is reduced.

Fixed-Price Method

Franchises and businesses selling certain products, such as automobiles, may be forced to sell their wares at prices fixed by the franchiser or manufacturer. Fixed pricing makes pricing strategy simple. The entrepreneur has no decision to make, other than whether the business can survive at the product's fixed price. Thus, while price may not be the key issue, the percent of net profit derived based on the price fixed by the manufacturer may make the franchise or dealership undesirable. Some organizations, such as automotive companies, permit their dealers to negotiate with a customer for the actual selling price as long as they use the manufacturer's list price as the starting point. This provides flexibility in the final net price and also avoids charges of price fixing.

"WG" Pricing Method

"WG" stands for "wild guess." No planning or analysis goes into the pricing. The person responsible intuitively feels a certain price is fair and then charges that price. Only later does he determine whether the price yields a reasonable profit.

Many businesses with a minimal understanding of accounting use the WG method. It is very common in service industries, when the owner is uncertain what the service is worth or costs and guesses a reasonable price for it. Many businesses do not even keep records that indicate how much product is consumed in providing a service. Some owners are happy with their pricing policy as long as the bank keeps cashing their checks.

Competitive Pricing

Another common pricing strategy is to price products competitively with other similar businesses in your field. Many businesses regularly visit or call competitors to find out their rates for similar services or products. Many small businesses use their friends and families to determine the competitor's price. They then establish prices equal to, or lower than, their competitors'.

This strategy works exceptionally well when small businesses are competing with national counterparts. For example, assume you wanted to open a local fast-food restaurant to compete with a national chain. The local business recognizes it is not necessary to pay a franchise fee, and thus they can undersell the national fast-food chain and still make the same profit; assuming, of course, they get the same volume of business and other costs are equal.

The competitive pricing strategy is most effective when it is difficult for the customer to distinguish between products of two competitors. For example, when buying gasoline, the customer may not be able to differentiate between the quality of two competing brands. In those instances, price may be a very important variable and so a gas-station owner should know what its competitors are charging. A small difference may not be important, but a significant one may cause a large shift in customers from one business to another.

Purchase Price Plus Overhead

If the product is purchased and marketed, the cost to acquire the product is known. The business can then increase price to cover overhead costs and hopefully provide itself with a reasonable profit. The success of this method may depend on the careful selection of the margin added to the purchase price of the product.

Let's examine a typical retail store. The owner purchases products from a variety of vendors and sells them to the public. Let us further assume that the owner of the store has decided that a 50 percent markup would be reasonable. Therefore, if the owner purchased product X for $10 he will sell that product for $15.

The markup percentage can be the generally accepted markup for the industry, but the owner should always analyze the cost of operating his business and then determine what percentage of estimated sales that represents. If it costs the owner $30,000 a year to run his store and he believes he can sell a quantity of product that would cost him $100,000, then he would need a 30 percent markup ($30,000 operating cost is 30 percent of the $100,000 purchase price of the product) to break even. The owner then adds what he believes is a realistic profit; for example, if the owner wants to make $20,000 profit then his markup should be 50 percent ($30,000 cost plus $20,000 profit is 50 percent of the $100,000 purchase price). In other words, every product that costs the owner a dollar should be sold for $1.50 to achieve the profitability objective.

Cost to Produce Plus

This method is basically the same as the purchase-price-plus method just described. The difference is that the cost of the product is the cost to manufacture as opposed to the cost to purchase. While the cost to purchase is known, the cost to manufacture may be significantly more difficult to determine.

Costs that should be included in the cost to manufacture include:

- Cost of direct labor.
- Cost of direct supplies.
- Cost to guarantee or repair defective products.
- Cost of the plant and equipment used to make the product.
- Cost of utilities to operate the equipment.
- Cost of indirect labor.

Note that indirect labor should include all of the plant-supervision and support services involved in making the product.

Because these costs are based on estimated production it is important to estimate the number of items that will be produced properly. This has a significant bearing on the selling price of the product. For example, if it costs $25,000 to run the plant, that $25,000 overhead is divided among the number of products made. If only one product is made per year, the cost of that product would be the $25,000 plus the direct material and labor. On the other hand, if two products were made, then only $12,500 would be allocated to each product for manufacturing overhead, while if 25,000 products were made the overhead would only be $1 per product. You can see how significantly the selling prices of the products will vary.

Desired Percent of Profit

This is the most logical method for pricing a product, although it may not always be competitively possible. The concept is that you estimate your desired percent of profit on the basis of expected volume of sale. If sales drop below the expected level, so will profits, but if sales are greater than expected, profits will exceed expectations.

The expected level of profit should be consistent with the industry in which you operate. This is not to imply that you shouldn't strive for the upper end of the profit range but, rather, that you should be consistent with other similar businesses so that your pricing policy makes you competitive.

Under this method, calculate all of the costs of operating your business, then divide by the number of products you hope to sell. If you have many products the mathematics becomes more difficult, but the concept is the same. Let's assume that you intend to sell 5,000 products per year. The cost to obtain those products is $150,000, and the administrative and overhead costs to run the business are $50,000. Thus, you have a total cost for the year of $200,000. If you want to make a 25 percent profit you would have to generate revenue of $250,000 (25 percent of the $200,000 cost is $50,000; total income equals $250,000). You then divide the 5,000 products into the $250,000 and get a $5 selling price per product.

ESTABLISHING PRODUCT PRICES

Business people should take the following steps in developing a price for their product:

- *Step 1: Determine pricing strategy.* The business should

determine which of the pricing strategies is most appropriate. The most practical method is to determine the percent of net profit that you desire to achieve from your business. If a business person cannot obtain a reasonable profit, he should reevaluate his desire to continue in that business.
- *Step 2: Gather pricing information.* Each of the methods requires the business to gather pricing information. The type of information will vary depending on the strategy selected.
- *Step 3: Make pricing assumptions.* Several of the methods require revenue and cost projections. These numbers can be obtained from budgets or owner projections. You may need your accountant's assistance here.
- *Step 4: Calculate price.* Using the selected pricing methods, calculate product prices for the ensuing period.
- *Step 5: Challenge the price.* After the price has been calculated, the owner should challenge its validity. The pricing strategy is a guideline for developing a tentative price. If the owner believes the price is either too high or too low, adjustments should be made.

PRICING CONSIDERATIONS

In calculating or challenging the price of your products, consider the following:

Reasonable profit. Pricing methods that do not result in a reasonable profit should be discarded. Businesses should reward their owners for their efforts unless there is a conscious decision to price for other considerations. I have worked with one organization that has been pricing their services at a break-even point in order to establish their reputation. Unfortunately, the business has been operating this way for so long it now seems unable to increase prices because it has established an expectation of low price with its clients.

Identify all *costs*. Know your expenditures and know what costs are associated with what products. Pricing is too important to leave to chance. If you neglect to identify all the product costs, you may be selling products at a loss.

Identify administrative costs. An important part of your pricing strategy is spreading the cost of running your business over the total number of products sold. Don't be overly impressed by figures for gross profits; the bottom line is the only profit that really counts.

Identify realistic sales estimates. Price should depend directly on the volume of products sold. If your sales estimates are unrealistic, you may lose money on a pricing strategy reflecting those unrealistic estimates. Use an estimate you are sure you can meet; if you exceed it enjoy the extra profits.

QUESTIONS ABOUT REASONABLE PROFIT

If you are unsure about what is a reasonable profit for your business, ask your accountant:

QUESTION: What is a reasonable profit for a business in my industry?
CONSIDERATIONS: Profits vary significantly from industry to industry. For example the retail food industry only makes two to three percent net profit, while the micro electronic industry has made over twenty percent net profit. Accountants have access to average gross and net profits for businesses by industry. You should obtain profit figures for your industry. These average figures can be helpful both for comparing your revenues and expenses against the norm and for establishing prices for your products.
QUESTION: What percent of profit am I making on my product sales today?
CONSIDERATIONS: Many different revenues and expenditures can be included in your financial statements. What you must

know is the gross and net profit made on each product or product line. In performing this analysis, you may find you are selling some products at a very high profit, while other products are being sold at a loss. There is nothing wrong with this if it is your intention to include some loss leaders, but you should at least be making a conscious decision to do so.

QUESTION: What has my profit-percentage trend been during the most recent year and the past five years?

CONSIDERATIONS: An important piece of information in your pricing strategy is your product-profit trend. If you are maintaining your profit levels over a period of time, that is fine, but if your profit levels are decreasing you should be concerned. Also, if your profit percentage is increasing you should be concerned with whether your sales volume is decreasing.

COST IDENTIFICATION QUESTIONS

If you are uncertain as to what costs should be included in your gross profit percentage, you should ask your accountant:

QUESTION: Can I identify product costs from my accounting records?

CONSIDERATIONS: The survival of a business hinges upon its ability to sell products at prices higher than it costs the business to acquire or produce them. If your accounting system cannot identify costs associated with specific products, your pricing policy will be a "wild guess" policy, not a planned policy. Some accounting systems are sensitive enough to associate costs with specific products, while others cannot. Your accountant can tell you if your accounting system can itemize costs at the product, or product-line, level.

QUESTION: Have I identified all of the product costs in my pricing calculation?

CONSIDERATIONS: Your accountant should review your pricing calculation. If you have overlooked areas of cost, he should be able to identify them so your pricing strategy will be more accurate.

QUESTION: Is my product cost increasing or decreasing?

CONSIDERATIONS: If your costs are changing it may be necessary to adjust your prices accordingly. An analysis of your financial records over a period of time will tell you the trend of your product costs, which will help you project costs and adjust prices for the next year.

QUESTION: Are there quantity levels that, when reached, will cause my costs to change significantly?

CONSIDERATIONS: Rarely do costs increase directly with the quantity of products purchased or produced. There are certain levels, or break points, where quantity discounts can significantly reduce costs, and there are other points where your existing plant and equipment may not be able to handle your volume. Moving to facilities that can handle larger volumes can create substantial increases in costs at particular levels. These cost breaks need to be anticipated and included in your pricing strategy.

QUESTIONS ABOUT ADMINISTRATIVE COSTS

If you are uncertain about the impact administrative costs have on your pricing strategy, you should ask your accountant:

QUESTION: How much would it cost to operate my business even if I could not sell any products?

CONSIDERATIONS: Businesses incur costs just by existing. If you rent your facility, you must pay the landlord, whether or not you make any sales. As an entrepreneur you should know your minimum fixed costs. Obviously, these must be recouped before you can make a profit.

QUESTION: Is there an easy method of obtaining cost figures for pricing purposes?

CONSIDERATIONS: If approximate cost figures are sufficient (and they usually are) there are easy methods to develop them. If products are purchased, first determine the cost to buy each product, which can be obtained from the vendor; then multiply it by business costs expressed as a percentage cost of products sold for the previous accounting period. For example, if, during the last accounting period $50,000 of inventory was sold, and $40,000 of costs were incurred in selling those products, the percentage to be used would be 80 percent (i.e., $40,000 is 80 percent of $50,000). Thus, an easy way to estimate the cost to use in developing a selling price for a product would be to use 180 percent of the purchase price as the break-even cost. If products are manufactured, the cost to manufacture a product is substituted for the cost to buy a product.

QUESTIONS ABOUT SALES ESTIMATES

If you have concerns over the reasonableness of your sales estimates, you should ask your accountant:

QUESTION: Is my business's pricing strategy realistic?
CONSIDERATIONS: The objective of a pricing strategy is to develop competitive prices that will return a fair profit for your effort. The method you select should, first, be competitive with other similar businesses in your community and, second, provide you with a profit that compensates you for your time and investment in your business. Your strategy is realistic if you are generating the amount of profit that satisfies you.
QUESTION: What effect would a 10 percent increase or decrease in my sales volume have on my expected profit?
CONSIDERATIONS: Your pricing strategy should include contingency planning for the impact of changes in sales volume. If a small downward shift in sales could destroy your profit margins, recalculate your product prices using a slightly lower sales volume. It is safer to be conservative, if marketing conditions permit it.

QUESTION: Are my product prices reasonable?

CONSIDERATIONS: Your accountant is not a marketing expert, but he can assess your recommended prices on the basis of his knowledge of the particular industry, your past business experience, and his review of the financial records of similar businesses. The accountant's insight may help you avoid losing business because of overpricing or losing profitability unnecessarily because of underpricing your products.

QUESTION: Is my business losing money on any product or product line?

CONSIDERATIONS: It is important to know which are your most profitable and least profitable products. It would be unfortunate to put major marketing efforts into selling products that are losing money or making minimal profits while putting minimal marketing effort into selling the higher-profit products. Many marketing strategies offer certain products at minimal or no profit, but they do so with the knowledge that they are loss leaders.

QUESTION: Which costs are most affected by volume?

CONSIDERATIONS: Profitability can be increased by reducing costs as a percent of sales. If the owner knows what costs are most affected by volume, he can calculate the effect on profits of volume changes. This may cause him to initiate a discount policy to promote quantity sales. The business should estimate the correlation between each individual cost item to the sales of a product. For example, the cost of the product might continue to show a 100 percent correlation to sales: meaning that a product's price is $2, and it costs $2 for each sale. On the other hand, rent may show a 0 percent correlation. Knowing these correlations will tell the owner how profitability can increase with volume, and what the impact on profit will be of reducing specific costs. For example, reducing the cost of products 5 percent is normally much more valuable than reducing rent by 5 percent.

QUESTION: What are the major costs in obtaining and selling my products?

CONSIDERATIONS: Management must continually attempt to identify and reduce product costs. The maximum benefit can be derived from reducing the larger costs. For example, if the cost of product X is 90 percent labor and 10 percent materials a much greater saving can be achieved by reducing labor 10 percent than can be achieved by reducing material costs 10 percent.

QUESTION: How frequently should I change my prices?

CONSIDERATIONS: There are two reasons to change product prices: first, the cost to obtain or sell the product changes; second, market conditions force a product price change. The accountant cannot advise you on market conditions, but he can advise you when there has been a significant change in product costs or marketing costs. These changes may be due to changing sales volume or changing costs. Businesses should continually monitor their products' sales volumes and costs so they know when it is necessary to make a pricing change to obtain a reasonable profit.

CHAPTER 9
Satisfying Regulatory Requirements

GOVERNMENT red tape saps the blood of many businesses: we work about five months a year just to earn sufficient funds to pay our taxes. Some business people facetiously say they spend the rest of the year filling out governmental forms to give the money to the government.

A recent article described one large pharmaceutical company that actually filled several large tractor-trailers with paperwork in order to comply with the federal requirements for the issuance of a new drug. One can visualize Washington slowly sinking into the Potomac under the weight of completed federal forms. Nor should one underestimate state, provincial, and local governments in their quest to compete with the federal government in terms of forms to complete. There are government subcultures that actually specialize in the creation of forms!

REQUIREMENTS FOR STARTING A BUSINESS

An entrepreneur wanting to go into business finds a location, identifies and obtains his product, devises a marketing program, locates customers, and begins selling. That's the business side of establishing a business. Anyone can do that.

Let's look at how a business is really begun. The entrepreneur consults a lawyer and an accountant to determine the firm's organizational structure. If a corporate structure is selected, forms are completed and sent to the state for processing. The entrepreneur applies to the Internal Revenue Service for a tax number. The local municipality wants an occupation fee, the county municipalities want informational forms. You can't hire people without filing the necessary tax-withholding forms, and on and on. Note that what really happens bears little resemblance to what should happen.

Without proper counseling and advice, the small-business person can become so entangled in trying to understand and comply with regulations that the important part of his business effort goes awry. Let's list and describe some of the regulatory requirements for establishing a business:

- *Tax identification number.* Each business must obtain from the federal government an identifying number for taxing purposes.
- *Employee withholding forms.* Special forms and cards need to be obtained so appropriate taxes can be withheld from employee wages and submitted to the appropriate collection agency, usually a bank.
- *Sales-tax forms.* Businesses selling products to customers need to collect and report sales tax to the appropriate agency. In addition, the funds need to be deposited in a bank or remitted directly to the appropriate agency.
- *Occupancy license.* Some municipalities require a business to get an occupancy license before it can occupy business premises.
- *Corporate registration.* The creation of a corporation, like the birth of a child, must be registered with the state before the rights of the corporation are recognized. This usually involves a fee.

- *Head tax.* Some municipalities charge a tax for each worker in the organization.
- *Business-privilege tax.* Some municipalities tax companies for the privilege of conducting business within their municipality.
- *Property and inventory tax.* Organizations may need to establish and file the estimated value of their property and/or inventory. One taxing district may tax inventory, while another taxes property. These are frequently called tangible and intangible property taxes.
- *Unemployment taxes.* Organizations are required to apply for an unemployment tax rate when they go into business. This rate will be adjusted according to their record of hiring and firing.

ONGOING BUSINESS REQUIREMENTS

Most of the forms, taxes, and fees associated with organizing a company continue throughout its life. For example, if it is necessary to file a corporate fee to register the firm, there is probably an annual renewal fee. The same holds true for most other forms required by taxing districts. In most taxing districts the initial filing puts the business on the mailing list so the business will automatically receive the appropriate tax forms year after year.

The good news is that there are always new regulations with which a business must comply in addition to all the initial and repeated filings. The first forms are primarily for taxing agencies; the ongoing requirements usually relate to the operation of the business. Some of the ongoing regulations that require compliance, although not always forms, include:

- *Federal wage and hour laws.* These govern minimum and overtime wages for employees.
- *Fire requirements.* Many businesses are required to mark

fire exits and place fire extinguishers in strategic locations.
- *Equal opportunity employment.* Many employment requirements are designed to eliminate discrimination because of race, sex, handicap, religion, or age.
- *Occupational safety and health.* Organizations may be required to comply with safety and health requirements. These govern the type of safety features needed on equipment, plant exits, lighting, noisy machinery and so forth.
- *Corporate minutes.* Corporations must periodically hold meetings of their boards of directors in order to satisfy state requirements. In some instances, the date and time of the corporate meeting must be provided to the stockholders several days or weeks in advance of the actual meeting.
- *Pricing policies.* Some businesses are required to sell products at the same price to the same type of customer. In addition, government contractors may be required to sell their products to the government at the lowest price they offer to any of their customers.

CEASING OPERATIONS

Just as a business can't open its doors and start selling a product, neither can it just shut its doors and cease to exist. Corporations are more complex to dissolve than are sole proprietorships. All of the interaction that is started when the business begins must be canceled when the business closes. This process may involve filing a series of final tax forms. For example, sales tax may be owed, federal withholding taxes may be held in escrow and may need to be deposited in banks, and business income taxes may be due.

The cessation process for a business may continue for many months after the business has stopped selling. For example, employees require end-of-year statements supporting their withholding taxes, and these must be prepared and disseminated to employees within a specified time period. Many taxing authorities require annual reports covering business operations during the preceding calendar or fiscal year. These must be completed and returned to the appropriate taxing agency.

Business people do not need to make plans on how to dissolve but a person should recognize the complexity of terminating a business, should he decide to do so. Lawyers and accountants may be required to satisfy all of the taxing requirements.

SUGGESTED METHOD FOR SATISFYING LEGAL REQUIREMENTS

If you haven't been in business before, the regulatory paperwork will both amaze and frustrate you. Nevertheless, you must try to comply with regulations while at the same time minimizing the effort expended on doing so. Failure to comply with most regulations results in sanctions and penalties. Noncompliance can be extremely costly and in many instances is cumulative. In other words, penalties accumulate each day that the business is not in compliance with the regulation. Businesses must avoid these penalties whenever possible.

The following approach is recommended to aid businesses in coping with federal, state, and local regulations:

Step 1. Consult the experts. Business owners should consult individuals knowledgeable in federal, state, and local regulations to identify all those requiring compliance. This step is for fact gathering: to gain an understanding of the effort required to complete forms, and to know the costs involved and the penalties for noncompliance. The types of experts you may want to consult include:

- Lawyers.
- Accountants.
- Regulatory agencies.

Step 2. List regulatory compliance characteristics. A worksheet (see Figure 5) should be prepared showing all of the tasks required for the business to be in compliance with regulations. Tasks should be listed in calendar sequence. The owner can use this as a "to-do" list to ensure that all of the functions are completed by the specified date.

Step 3. Assign a responsible individual. The owner should determine who is the best individual to oversee the performance of the tasks. Commonly this will be the accountant, the lawyer, or someone in the business.

Figure 5

REGULATORY COMPLIANCE CHECKLIST

Areas (Agency Responsible)	Task	Due Date	Assigned to	Completed by	Date
Federal corporate income tax (U.S. government)	File annual return	4/15	Joe		
	File estimated tax return	4/15	Joe		
	Pay 1st quarter estimated tax	4/15	Mary		
	Pay 2nd quarter estimated tax	6/15	Mary		
	Pay 3rd quarter estimated tax	9/15	Mary		
	Pay 4th quarter estimated tax	1/15	Mary		

Areas (Agency Responsible)	Task	Due Date	Assigned to	Completed by	Date
Unemployment taxes (state)	File annual state return	6/15	Tom		
	Pay 1st quarter tax	6/15	Mary		
	Pay 2nd quarter tax	9/15	Mary		
	Pay 3rd quarter tax	12/15	Mary		
	Pay 4th quarter tax	3/15	Mary		
Occupancy fee (city government)	Pay occupancy fee to city	1/15	Jane		
Intangible tax (county government)	File and pay intangible tax	5/15	Steve		
Tangible tax (state government)	File and pay tangible tax	8/15	Steve		
Deposit FWT, FICA	Make deposit in bank	Monthly on 15th	Cindy		
Deposit sales tax (state government)	Make deposit in bank	Monthly on 15th	Esther		

REGULATORY BENEFITS

For every bit of darkness, there is a glimmer of light. Occasionally, businesses can obtain some financial benefit from regulations. Companies should be aware of these opportunities, even though they may decide not to take advantage of them.

Most relate to special business tax breaks. The more common tax breaks include:

- *Creating jobs.* Special tax benefits may be available if the business creates new jobs. For example, if you had three employees last year and add a fourth this year, you may be eligible for a tax break because your business created a new job.
- *Hiring the handicapped.* Special tax credits may be available if you choose to hire handicapped individuals. Business experience with handicapped workers has generally been highly favorable, and the tax benefits may make this a desirable option.
- *Business location.* In order to attract businesses, many municipalities provide incentives ranging from free land and low-interest loans to exemptions from property tax to businesses that locate in their area. In economically depressed areas, the federal and state governments may provide similar benefits.

REGULATORY CONSIDERATIONS

Compliance with regulations is an essential part of conducting business. There is no choice about compliance, but the methods of doing so can vary. The points to consider in how you fulfill regulatory requirements are:

- *Time.* Businesses should attempt to comply with regulations while minimizing the amount of time and effort expended to do so.

- *Cost.* Businesses should attempt to minimize the amount of funds spent on compliance. Funds are expended in performing the tasks necessary for compliance as well as in actually paying the taxes and fees.
- *Benefit.* Businesses should consider and take advantage of regulatory benefits helpful to the operation of their business.

CHAPTER HIGHLIGHT

Get on top of regulatory requirements quickly and then prepare a work schedule that ensures compliance with them.

Time Questions

In an effort to reduce the amount of time businesses expend on complying with regulations, you may wish to ask your accountant:

QUESTION: Will regulatory agencies help my business comply with regulations?
CONSIDERATIONS: Yes, some agencies, such as the U.S. Internal Revenue Service, have "starter kits" for new businesses. All agencies provide directions on how to complete the forms needed to satisfy their requirements. In addition, some private businesses, such as Commerce Clearing House, sell manuals on compliance to specific regulations. See Appendix A for a listing of resources.
QUESTION: Where do I obtain the information I need to complete government forms?
CONSIDERATIONS: A business's accounting system should be designed to provide the information needed to complete govern-

ment forms. Most information is required periodically, which makes interim analyses uneconomical. If the information is needed on a regular basis, it should be produced by the business's accounting system. In addition, the firm should have the previous year's tax form available so permanent information, such as your business code, date of incorporation, and so on can be copied directly from the previous form.

QUESTION: Who should be responsible for compliance with various government regulations?

CONSIDERATIONS: If possible, the people responsible for the areas covered by the forms should complete them. For example, the individual responsible for preparing the payroll should prepare the governmental forms relating to the payroll. Thus, the individual most experienced in the area obtains and prepares information.

QUESTION: What forms should be prepared by my accountant?

CONSIDERATIONS: Forms for compliance that employees of the business do not understand or are confused by. In other words, business people should prepare all they can, leaving to the accountant the more complex and unusual forms. For example, most businesses have their accountant prepare their annual business income tax returns but not their monthly or quarterly payroll deposit forms.

QUESTION: Should I take the time necessary to ensure that my return is accurate and complete?

CONSIDERATIONS: Much can be done to simplify the preparation of government forms, but that should not include submitting inaccurate or incomplete information. The governmental agency to whom the form is sent will probably request any missing information and may challenge inaccurate information. It is generally worth the time and effort to do the forms right the first time.

QUESTION: How can I complete forms I don't understand?

CONSIDERATIONS: Your accountant should be familiar with all of the financial forms you need to complete to be in compliance with government regulations. If the forms are repetitive, it is normally easier for someone from the business to complete them than to ask your accountant to do it. However, you can work with your accountant on one or two iterations in order to learn how to fill it out properly.

COMPLIANCE QUESTIONS

If you are concerned about compliance with governmental regulations, you may wish to ask your accountant:

QUESTION: How will I know I am complying with all appropriate regulations?
CONSIDERATIONS: Prepare a list that identifies the tasks required. If you complete all of the items on the prescribed date you will have a high degree of assurance that you are in compliance with government regulations.
QUESTION: What will happen if I file my returns late or make an error on a form?
CONSIDERATIONS: The penalty for noncompliance or error varies depending on the agency involved. In some instances you will receive a warning; in others you may be penalized. The instructions explaining compliance normally set forth penalties for noncompliance or error.
QUESTION: If I receive a penalty for noncompliance can I appeal it?
CONSIDERATIONS: Many businesses have successfully appealed penalties. It is common, when establishing a new business, not to receive all the necessary forms in time to fulfill all regulations. Until you have the forms, you can't comply. Therefore, a letter explaining the situation is normally acceptable to the regulatory agency and the penalty will be dropped. If this happens to you, consider having your accountant write the letter.
QUESTION: If I don't know that I have to prepare certain forms, will I be held responsible for noncompliance?

CONSIDERATIONS: Ignorance of the law is no excuse. When you organize your business you are responsible for knowing and fulfilling the applicable regulations, and thus are responsible as well for noncompliance. This is why it is important to identify all of the appropriate regulations early in your business life.

QUESTION: How long should I save information supporting the forms and returns submitted to regulatory agencies?

CONSIDERATIONS: As a general rule, save copies of *all* tax returns for seven years, and supporting information for three full calendar years following the year you report the information. It is advisable to consult an accountant or lawyer before deciding on the retention period for financial documents.

QUESTION: If I don't have time to complete the return or have not accumulated the necessary information by the form's due date, can I get an extension?

CONSIDERATIONS: Most businesses can get extensions if they have a valid reason. In some cases, it is not even necessary to state the reason for filing late; extensions for limited periods of time are often available for the asking. Normally, though, it is necessary to estimate any amounts due and pay them on the due date, even though the paperwork will follow by several weeks or months.

QUESTION: How will I know when regulations change?

CONSIDERATIONS: Most government agencies issue pamphlets and instructions on changing regulations. In addition, many accounting firms have a newsletter for their clients reporting changes and what the clients must do to comply. One question you should be asking your accountant every year is, "What are the changes in government regulations that affect my business, how do the changes affect it, and how do I comply with them?"

COST CONSIDERATIONS

Questions you can ask your accountant about minimizing the cost of regulations include:

QUESTION: Are there ways to reduce the fees and taxes I must pay?
CONSIDERATIONS: There are many ways to avoid taxes (see Chapter 6 for more information). In addition, the amount of your tax or fee frequently can be reduced if the taxing district offers discounts for early payment. For example, many property-tax assessments offer early-payment discounts that can reduce the tax burden by a few percentage points.
QUESTION: Are there ways to reduce the tangible-property taxes?
CONSIDERATIONS: Many tangible-property taxes are based on an assessment of the value of property on a specific date. If you know that date, you can take measures to reduce the amount of property on hand. For example, if the tangible property tax is based on an assessment as of December 31, you might let your inventory drop to its yearly low on that date before beginning to rebuild afterwards.
QUESTION: How can I reduce the cost of preparing required forms?
CONSIDERATIONS: Two options are to use employees of the business or to hire outside experts to help. The cost of preparing returns using both methods should be determined and the best alternative selected. In many cases, accountants using computers can prepare tax returns and forms much more cheaply than the business owner can manually.

BENEFIT QUESTIONS

If you feel you might be eligible for tax benefits, you may wish to ask your accountant these questions:

QUESTION: How can I keep informed about new government benefit programs?

CONSIDERATIONS: Your accountant should be able to advise you of new programs from which you can benefit. For example, changes in tax laws, new tax benefits for meeting specified conditions, and so on. You should expect your accountant to keep you advised on new or changed programs. Many accounting firms issue newsletters to their clients advising them of tax-benefit programs. Availability of this type of information from your accountant should be one of the criteria to use in selecting your accountant. In addition, the *Kiplinger Washington Letter* or similar publications are a good source of information.

QUESTION: Are there government agencies that provide information to businesses?

CONSIDERATIONS: Yes, and many of these are listed in Appendix A. A wealth of technical information is also available through the National Technical Information Service (NTIS), a part of the U.S. Department of Commerce, located at 5285 Port Royal Road, Springfield, VA 22161.

NTIS is an information service organization stemming from a congressionally created predecessor. It channels information about technological innovations and other specialized information to business, educators, government, and the public. Its products and services are intended to increase the efficiency and effectiveness of U.S. research and development, to support U.S. foreign policy goals by assisting the social and economic development of other nations, and to increase the availability of foreign technical information in the United States. NTIS undertakes and develops innovative information products and programs appropriate for government, but which have the potential to become self-supporting.

QUESTION: Should I contact my legislators for information and assistance on government programs?

CONSIDERATIONS: Don't overlook your elected legislators for information and assistance, both federal and state. It is generally a good idea to send a letter with the same wording to all your elected legislators explaining your business objectives and asking what government benefit programs would be of value to your business, and also asking how you might obtain government contracts for your business. It is also advisable to keep in contact with your elected legislators so you are continually advised by them of new programs and opportunities. You can obtain the names and addresses of your elected legislators from your local chamber of commerce or your telephone directory.

CHAPTER 10

Employees and Employee Benefits

EMPLOYEES are commonly—and mistakenly—thought of as a necessary evil. Unless you work by yourself, employees are, at least, necessary. Each should, however, be profitable in terms of the business. As a rule of thumb, hire competent people; fire incompetent people.

Employees can generate two kinds of problems: personnel-related and finance-related. Personnel problems are management problems outside the expertise of most accountants.

The financial difficulties associated with employees are in the areas of wages, benefits, and taxes. Only when you add all the costs can you determine whether your employees are generating a profit for your business. Your accountant can help you with these analyses and other employee and payroll considerations.

EMPLOYEES VERSUS CONTRACT WORKERS

Businesses have two options when it comes to personnel: they can hire individuals as employees of the business; or they can hire contract workers. "Contract worker" is used here in the broad sense, as an individual doing work for you but not on staff, or a member of your organization. The word "contract" is used because most of these employees sign some kind of contract or agreement to perform work for compensation. An employee imposes more obligations on the employer than does the contract worker, but is normally better skilled and more loyal. Of course he is also available when you need him.

The difference is the obligation the business has to the person. A staff member makes a specified wage each week. It is immaterial whether the individual has been successful or not in that week. The wage is due and payable upon completion of the week's work.

A contract worker, on the other hand, is usually paid on the basis of actual time spent on a project, actual expenses directly incurred, or actual results. Most contract workers who sell are paid a commission on their sales and do not get a salary. If the contract worker sells fifty products a week, that individual will receive a predetermined commission on each sale. The more sales the contract worker makes the more he receives. Obviously, businesses can use both staff and contract workers depending on conditions.

Contracting Work

Using contract workers requires different managerial considerations than using employees. For example, management can quickly shift staff employees into new areas of need but may have to negotiate in order to change contract workers' workloads or time schedules. Normally contract workers negotiate the work they will perform, and requested deviations must be individually negotiated.

A business might want to use contract workers for the following reasons:

- *To obtain high-price skills.* The organization needs unique skills, such as those required for tax preparation, and cannot afford—or does not need—to hire people who possess such skills as employees.

- *To meet peak workloads.* The volume of business fluctuates significantly, and it is uneconomical to hire employees for peak loads and keep them busy during slack time.
- *To save money.* It may be cheaper to hire contract workers to do a job than to perform a job in-house. For example, organizations may find it cheaper to have their data processing done at service bureaus rather than purchasing a computer and the staff needed to develop systems to operate the computer.
- *To eliminate the need to supervise.* It may be necessary to perform functions in remote locations. For example, marketing personnel may be required in distant states. If employees are located in remote areas, they become difficult to supervise and control. The contract worker's role can be structured so his payment is dependent upon performance, thus the need for supervision is minimal.

The business's concern over contract workers is the development of the contract, which must be as specific as possible, since ambiguities usually lead to misinterpretations, which lead to problems. The benefit of using contract workers is lost if excessive time is spent interpreting and arguing over the meaning of the contract.

The information to be specified in a contract or agreement with an individual include:

- Effective date of the contract.
- Period of the contract.
- Place of business for conducting work.
- Type of support given the contract worker by the business, such as advertising, supplies, auto.
- Method and timing of compensation.
- Company's expectations of contract worker (e.g., sales quota).
- Penalties in the event contract worker fails to live up to expectation.

- Penalties in the event the business fails to live up to contractual obligations.
- Methods of terminating contract.
- Length of contract.
- Method of negotiating changes.
- Method for extending contract.

Finding and Keeping Employees

Finding and keeping competent employees is an ongoing challenge for businesses. Employees are attracted to a company because of the financial rewards and benefits, the challenge of the job, the potential for advancement, the location of the business, and a myriad of other personal considerations. It is important to have personnel policies that encourage good people to stay. The cost associated with poor policies can be extensive.

Most personnel policies are outside the scope of the accountant's role. Some accountants can provide a service by helping define the skills appropriate to various jobs and salary ranges, design, implement, and administer employee benefits. In some cases accountants help businesses find qualified individuals, especially accountants.

Prior to hiring an individual, a business should define the expectations of that position and establish a salary range for the job. If the position is directly related to the line of business, such as a cook in a restaurant, the owners should be able to describe the job and establish a salary range. On the other hand, if the position is not mainline, demanding an administrative or technical skill, for example, a secretary, billing clerk, key entry operator, the owners may not be familiar with either the skills required or the prevailing salary structure. The accountant can be most helpful in these areas.

Some accounting firms provide employment-agency services to their clients. It may be a formal service, in which they have an actual employment agency, or an informal service, where they become a clearinghouse for past employees of their firm or qualified individuals they know who are looking for a position. Depending on the formality of the service, an employment-agency fee may or may not be charged.

Employee benefits. Every employer will incur expenses above and beyond the salary paid to his employees. As a minimum, he will pay the employer's share of federal taxes on employees, such as unemployment and social security. In addition to these mandated benefits the employer may decide to provide voluntary benefits, which he may pay for fully or which may be paid for jointly by the employee and employer. The more common types of employee benefits are:

- Paid vacation.
- Paid holidays.
- Paid sickness.
- Hospital insurance.
- Dental insurance.
- Pension plans.
- Stock option plans (usually for management).

Owners of a small business frequently use the business to gain personal tax advantages on benefits. For example, when they participate in business benefit plans, such as pension plans, the owners' contributions can be paid for with pretax dollars. For individuals in high tax brackets, considerable savings can result.

When owners of a small business establish benefit plans, they usually (and rightly) consider their own personal gain from the plan. For example, an owner may want to establish a liberal retirement plan so he can retire early and live well. He should be aware, however, that plans developed for the business normally apply to all employees, not just himself. In other words, if the owners establish a liberal pension plan, all of the employees in the business are covered by the same pension plan, and that can lead to huge expenditures.

John Carson established a small business as a corporation. The only employees were members of John's family. The corporation immediately established a medical plan in which the corporation paid the full cost of the medical insurance for the employees, plus reimbursed the employees for all costs incurred by the employee above and beyond those covered by the medical plan. In other words, John had 100 percent medical coverage for himself and his family. The business grew and the corporation needed to hire employees outside of the immediate family. These new employees were covered by the same medical plan, which went unchanged. One of the employees got cancer and the medical expenses ran into many thousands of dollars above that covered by the medical insurance. The family corporation was required to reimburse that employee for all medical costs not covered by the medical insurance.

With sufficient planning and guidance, the scope of employee benefits can normally be tailored to achieve the objectives of the owner. For example, the owners of the business may decide they want a very liberal retirement plan but also recognize that they will have to include all the employees of the business in the plan. The owners may want to participate in the plan but may not want their employees covered. In this case, a retirement plan could be established that only covers employees with salary levels above the maximum social security salary. This would mean that the company makes no participation to the pension plan on salaries equal to or less than, the maximum salary subject to social security taxes, but for the portion of salaries above that limit the contribution can be large. In fact, the contribution might exceed the individual's salary, depending on his age and the type of plan.

There are three options in establishing pension programs:

1. *Individual Retirement Accounts (IRA).* Each eligible individual establishes an IRA account in his/her name. IRAs are for individuals under 70½ who have income from wages, salary, or fees. They can be established whether or not the individual participates in other pension programs or has a Keogh plan. The limit is currently $2,000 yearly for individuals, $4,000 for a working couple and $2,250 for a couple when only one is working.

2. *Keogh plans.* For proprietors and other self-employed persons. The current limit is 15 percent of earnings up to $15,000 per year. The benefits can be bigger for a "defined-benefits" program. Note that the two types of plans are contributory and have defined benefits. A contributory plan specifies the amount contributed to the plan, such as 15 percent of earnings. A defined-benefit plan specifies the desired benefit, such as 75 percent of current income at retirement, thus the contribution must be sufficient to provide that benefit.
3. *Pension plan.* A corporation establishes a pension plan specifically for its employees. Normally these plans are customized and can be either contributory or defined-benefit.

It should be noted that once they are established it may be difficult to reduce or eliminate benefit programs. Owners should investigate their option to make changes. For example, it is difficult to reduce pension plans once established, but not to increase benefits.

Retaining employees through benefit plans. The objective of voluntary benefit plans is to provide an incentive to retain good employees. If the plan ignores this principle, the gain to the owners may be negligible. For example, the business may decide not to give employees vacation for the first twelve months, or let them participate in pension plans for the first year or two in order to offer them an advantage for staying with the organization. Some businesses increase the percent of vesting in pension plans over an extended period of time. (Vesting means the portion of the value of the benefit owned by the employee.) For example, ten-year vesting means the first year an employee is with a company they only vest or own 10 percent of the value of their pension, the second year they vest 20 percent, the third 30 percent, and so on, for ten years, when they become fully vested. This provides an economic incentive for the employee to stay with the organization. If an employee leaves before being fully vested the unvested funds are returned to the plan.

Businesses should periodically assess the effectiveness of the benefit program in helping to keep employees. If the business is losing desirable staff members but keeping those employees of average or below-average skills, the benefit program should be evaluated and changed so the objectives of the program are achieved. Benefits that have proved effective in helping to retain key employees include:

- *Stock-option plans.* Normally for management, giving them the right to buy stock in the future at a predetermined price.
- *Profit sharing.* Employees (some or all) divide a predetermined percentage of the profit.
- *Bonuses.* Extra income normally given if some predetermined objective is achieved.
- *Gifts and travel.* Based upon meeting or exceeding predetermined quotas, such as a trip to Florida for the top salesperson of the year.

Note that most incentive benefit programs determine in advance what must be achieved in order to receive the incentive.

FUNDING BENEFITS/ EMPLOYEE WITHHOLDINGS

Businesses may have some options available in the method and timing of paying for employee benefits. The funding of some programs, especially those required by governments, is tightly controlled. Others, especially voluntary programs such as pension plans, give businesses some latitude in payment options.

There are two primary considerations related to paying for benefit programs. The first is the availability of funds. If the organization is short of money, it may wish to defer its payment.

Second, the business must consider the tax advantage of making the payment. If the business is in a period of high profitability, it may wish to pay benefit contributions in advance in order to take higher tax deductions in a given year. On the other hand, if yearly profits are low, the business may wish to defer payments until profits increase.

Establishment of most benefit programs creates an obligation on the part of the business: the question is not whether to pay; the question is when to pay. Consult your tax advisor about the tax consequences of early and late payments.

EMPLOYEES AND EMPLOYEE BENEFIT CONSIDERATIONS

For many, employees and employee benefits are the major costs of doing business. Firms should adopt procedures that enable them to optimize their employee costs, and accountants can advise their clients on how to do this.

The areas to be considered in employee relations are:

- *Employee obligations.* The commitments a business incurs when it hires someone.
- *Employee benefits.* The costs and value of providing benefits to employees.
- *Management benefits.* Providing benefits to management that are not provided to employees.
- *Custodian of funds.* The custodial responsibilities of businesses in collecting and holding employee-benefit funds and taxes.
- *Contract work.* Obligations incurred when a business chooses to have work performed under contract rather than by employees.
- *Reporting requirements.* Different approaches require varying amounts of regulatory reporting.

CHAPTER HIGHLIGHT

From the business viewpoint employee benefits should be designed to keep employees. Understand what the benefit program will do for your business before you establish the program.

EMPLOYEE OBLIGATION QUESTIONS

If you are concerned about your obligations to employees, ask your accountant:

QUESTION: What obligations does my business have to its employees?
CONSIDERATIONS: Both laws and conventions apply to employer-employee relations. Employers have an obligation to pay employees for work performed at agreed-upon rates. In addition, the employer has obligations to withhold taxes and to make employer contributions to certain programs, such as FICA and unemployment. Also, there are moral conventions that employers should follow, such as giving an employee reasonable notice before termination.
QUESTION: Can I hire any employee I choose?
CONSIDERATIONS: Generally, employers are free to hire the most qualified individual, assuming they don't violate equal employment opportunity regulations. In other words, businesses are not free to discriminate against prospective employees because of age, race, religion, or sex.
QUESTION: Can I fire unqualified employees at my discretion?
CONSIDERATIONS: Generally, employers are able to fire individuals at their discretion, assuming there is just cause. If firing is done to discriminate against an individual, he or she may be

able to gain restitution from the employer for unjustified job termination.

QUESTION: Am I liable for my employees' actions?

CONSIDERATIONS: Operating within their job descriptions, employees are normally able to incur obligations in the business's name. For example, an employee that travels could charge an airline ticket to your company. If this is a concern, consult your lawyer.

QUESTION: What types of liabilities might I incur as a result of employees' working in my place of business?

CONSIDERATIONS: If employees are injured on the job, particularly if injury is due to negligence on the part of the business or failure to undertake reasonable safety measures, the organization can be sued by the employee. There are workmen's-compensation plans available to businesses to compensate employees for injuries.

QUESTION: Where can I obtain information about business obligations to employees?

CONSIDERATIONS: The information needed can be obtained from the U.S. Department of Labor and from local or state employment offices.

EMPLOYEE-BENEFITS QUESTIONS

For concerns regarding employee benefits, you might ask your accountant:

QUESTION: Is it necessary for my business to provide benefits to employees?

CONSIDERATIONS: Benefits prescribed by the government, which normally cover retirement, disability, and unemployment, must be offered to employees. The government prescribes the rate to be paid by employees and employer, as well as the benefits.

QUESTION: How do I decide what additional benefits to offer my employees?

CONSIDERATIONS: Business people normally want to offer salaries and benefits equivalent to those of similar businesses in the area so their business will be competitive with others in attracting and keeping employees. Determine the benefits provided by your competitors, and then decide whether it is advantageous to offer your employees those benefits.

QUESTION: If I decide to offer benefits such as health or life insurance, to whom should I talk to determine the cost and value of the program?

CONSIDERATIONS: Accountants visit many organizations and have an appreciation of both the cost and value of various benefit programs. They can provide initial reaction to programs and the companies that service those programs. You should then discuss the plan with several vendors to find the program that best meets your needs.

QUESTION: If I decide on a certain benefit program, such as health insurance, will the rates be the same from all the vendors of those programs?

CONSIDERATIONS: The rates may vary significantly from one vendor to another. Rates depend on the number of people covered, the programs offered by that vendor, and the terms of the contract. Many businesses have experienced very low rates the first year of the program and then have had significant increases the following years. In other words, the insurance company may offer the program for one year as a loss leader, hoping to then recoup the loss by increasing the rates the following years. Ask for long-term rate guarantees.

QUESTION: What will cause my rates to change on benefit programs?

CONSIDERATIONS: Rates are generally affected by your claims experience. This is true in both mandatory and voluntary benefit programs. Generally, the more claims filed against the benefit program the higher the rates will be for the following rating period. For example, terminating a lot of employees in a short time period causes your unemployment-compensation insurance premiums to increase.

QUESTION: Can I change benefit-program vendors?

CONSIDERATIONS: Once you start benefit programs, there are normally disadvantages in changing from one vendor to another. For example, in health insurance there may be a waiting period for employees to gain certain benefits. Some vendors may waive those exclusions in order to get your business.

MANAGEMENT-BENEFIT CONSIDERATIONS

If you want to differentiate between employee and management benefits you may wish to ask your accountant:

QUESTION: Can the benefits provided to the owners and management be different from those given employees?
CONSIDERATIONS: Generally, benefits provided to management must be provided to all employees. However, benefits can be structured to take effect above a certain salary level.
QUESTION: Can I develop unique programs for management?
CONSIDERATIONS: Programs to exclude nonmanagement personnel can be developed if they are designed as compensation packages. For example, management can be offered stock-option programs and bonuses. When offered to one member of management the program generally must be offered to all members of management at that level.
QUESTION: Should I establish goals for my benefit programs?
CONSIDERATIONS: Yes, you should. If you don't establish goals for the program, you have no way to measure its effectiveness. If the benefit program fails to meet business objectives, you should reevaluate the program to determine methods for making it more effective.

CONSIDERATIONS OF BEING A CUSTODIAN OF FUNDS

If you are concerned about your obligations as a custodian of employee benefit funds, you should ask your accountant:

QUESTION: Is it necessary for me to segregate funds held for payment of mandatory benefit programs?

CONSIDERATIONS: It is usually not necessary to establish special accounts for funds withheld from employee wages or accounts to pay the employer's share of mandatory benefit programs. Failure to transfer those funds to the government at the appropriate time carries severe penalties. Once collected, those funds must be appropriately safeguarded and paid to the government.

QUESTION: Newspaper articles continually describe pension programs that are not fully funded. Does this mean I don't have to fund my pension plans?

CONSIDERATIONS: When a business establishes a pension program, it has an obligation to fund that program. Many organizations do not have sufficient monies available to make their current contributions. There are, however, many different ways of funding that can satisfy the employer's immediate obligation to the program but not provide suffcent funds to pay employee benefits. When you establish pension plans you need to fully define both your short-range and long-range obligations and be sure to meet them.

QUESTION: If I am short of funds, can I borrow against monies designated for benefit programs, or delay payments to the fund?

CONSIDERATIONS: The structure of the benefit program outlines your flexibility in funding it. In general you cannot borrow against funds already paid into a benefit program, but you may be able to delay additional payments.

QUESTION: Are there tax advantages in timing benefit payments to occur in one year or the next?

CONSIDERATIONS: Businesses frequently have flexibility regarding the taxable year in which they wish to accrue certain benefits. Assuming you fulfill all legal requirements and obligations of the benefit program, you should make payments in the taxable year that gives you the most advantageous result.

CONTRACT WORKER CONSIDERATIONS

If you intend to hire contract workers, you might wish to ask your accountant:

QUESTION: What obligation does my business have to contract workers?
CONSIDERATIONS: If you contract out your work rather than hire staff your obligations are those specified in the contract.
QUESTION: How important is it to have a written contract with people working for me on a contract basis?
CONSIDERATIONS: Many people have standardized methods for performing work. For example, your lawyer and accountant are professionals whose work must conform to professional codes of ethics. Employment agencies and temporary-service groups usually provide rate structures for their employees' work. Other groups, such as service bureaus, may negotiate to perform certain tasks at predetermined fees. The formality of the process will vary. A formal contract provides you with greater protection for restitution, but in reality the quality of work is a function of the professionalism and good faith of the individual you are dealing with. If you have major concerns, consult your lawyer.
QUESTION: If I am unhappy with an employee's performance I can fire that individual; how do I get rid of a contract worker?
CONSIDERATIONS: The degree of difficulty of breaking a contract is determined by the specifications of the contract itself. Most informal working arrangements can be broken by either party with reasonable notice, but more formal contracts should contain provisions for termination.

CHAPTER 11
Surviving Cash Flow

CASH roulette is a game in which you keep one step ahead of the bill collector. If you win, you get to keep playing. If you lose, you go bankrupt. Cash management is not appreciated until cash is short. At that point it's normally too late to manage. Then you can only try to avoid disaster.

For one small business the make-or-break point of each day was the arrival of the mailman. The entire office staff would wait in anticipation, hoping a client had paid for services rendered. If funds came in, employees could be paid back wages and the business could catch up on bills. On the other hand, a day without money in the mailbox was a gloomy one indeed.

Businesses need to plan their flow of cash. And cash management must be made an integral part of the management process. Businesses can affect their cash receipts and can gain significant income from the proper use of excess cash.

MANAGEMENT OF CASH

Managing cash is in itself a small business. In fact, some businesses make more from their money-management operations than they do from the normal operation of their businesses. Insurance companies are excellent examples; frequently they lose money on underwriting but make significant profits on the prudent investment of premiums.

The cash manager of the business is normally the treasurer. His or her cash-management functions include:

- *Preparing cash budgets.* Statements are needed that indicate the supply and demand for cash during the next accounting period.
- *Monitoring.* Overseeing that the receipts and expenditures are within expectations.
- *Collections.* If collections lag behind expectations, procedures are invoked to improve the flow of funds.
- *Investments.* Cash surpluses should be invested to earn money for the business.
- *Crisis management.* If the business is in cash trouble, the manager needs to juggle revenue and short-term loans and delay expenditures to avert financial disaster.

CASH MANAGEMENT STATEMENTS

The cash manager uses two cash-analysis statements. A cash budget shows the projected inflow of cash from sales, investments and other activities, and the expected use of that cash for expenditures, capital purchases, payroll, and taxes. A working-capital statement shows how cash is generated and used by the business.

The cash-budget statement is actually a cash-flow projection. Note that the cash flow is different from the actual revenue. One is a process; one a tangible asset. What one must do is estimate the

Figure 6

CASH-BUDGET STATEMENT
FIRST QUARTER, 19XX

Estimated Cash Revenue	January	February	March	Total First Quarter
Payment of accounts receivable	$ 8,000	$ 9,000	$ 7,000	$24,000
Cash sales	1,000	3,000	2,000	6,000
Interest	—	—	1,000	1,000
Other	—	—	—	—
Revenue	$ 9,000	$12,000	$10,000	$31,000

Estimated Expenditures				
Salaries	2,000	2,000	2,000	6,000
Rent	1,000	1,000	1,000	3,000
Utilities	1,000	1,000	1,000	3,000
Advertising	1,000	1,000	2,000	4,000
Taxes	—	—	1,000	1,000
Payables	5,000	6,000	1,000	12,000
Other	—	—	—	—
Disbursements	$10,000	$11,000	$ 8,000	$29,000
Change in cash, current period	$ −1,000	$ 1,000	$ 2,000	$ 2,000
Change in cash, cumulative	$ −1,000	—	$ 2,000	$ 2,000

timing of cash payments to the company (the flow or process) and the amount (the tangible asset). Just because people owe money does not mean it will be paid on time.

Figure 6 is a cash-budget statement. During January the business had a negative cash flow; during the other two months of the quarter it had a positive cash flow. Note that the cash-budget statement differs completely from an income statement. The former reflects the movement of cash in and out of the business; the latter reflects both revenue and expenditures, of which cash is only one component.

Figure 7 is an example of a working-capital statement, which shows the sources and uses of funds during an accounting period. It too differs from the income and expense statement. Except for businesses operating on a cash basis, neither income nor expenditure need be a result of receiving or spending cash. Note that many items in the working-capital statement do not appear on the statement of income and expense.

Depreciation is a major source of cash for many businesses. When you buy an asset you may pay for it when you buy it or during its early years of life, getting the benefit of an expense long after you have paid for the asset. Let's assume you buy an automobile for $3,000 cash this year, and the auto will last for three years. If you take a $1,000 depreciation each year, you will spend $3,000 the first year but only get a deduction of $1,000. During the second and third year the deduction of $1,000 each year for automobile depreciation will generate cash that year because it is an expense for which the money was expended during the previous year (thereby saving cash outlays). For the same reason the purchase of an asset is a drain on cash because money is spent for which no deduction can be taken during the year the cash is expended.

Figure 7

Working-Capital Statement
For the Year Ended December 31, 19XX

Item	Use	Source	Balance
Opening working capital	——	——	$15,000
Purchase of capital assets	$ 6,000	——	——
Depreciation	——	$ 5,000	——
Sale of stock	——	8,000	——
Business profit	——	9,000	——
Dividend	8,000	——	——
	$14,000	$22,000	$15,000
Add increases to working capital			22,000
Subtract uses of working capital			14,000
Final working-capital balance			$23,000

CASH COLLECTIONS

Except for cash-only businesses, the collection of receivables from customers is a full-time job. It is good business to operate on other people's money, and companies can substantially increase their investment income by delaying payment to their vendors.

The management of accounts receivable involves:

- Carefully selecting credit risks.
- Monitoring the receipt of receivables.
- Taking action on overdue accounts.

When collections start to lag, or additional cash is needed, the cash manager can instigate any or all of the following cash collection techniques:

Offer credit customers a discount for paying cash. Some businesses give a 5 percent cash discount, which encourages the account to pay cash rather than charge the item. Normally, cash—as investment income—plus fewer bad debts, covers the cost of giving the discount.

Stop selling product to delinquent accounts. Establish a deadline after which a customer's account will be considered delinquent. At that point, stop selling additional product until the account is current. Again, it is better to lose a sale than a collection.

Bug the client. Make a pest out of yourself if you want the money quickly. Remember, they are the delinquent ones who should be concerned about the status of their credit.

Pressure, pressure, and pressure again. Use lawyers, collection agencies, or everyday pressuring letters from your business to provide an incentive to customers to pay their bills.

Sell your accounts receivable to a collection agency (factoring). Many collection agencies will buy receivables at a predetermined percent on the dollar. The percent received can vary significantly, depending on the age of the receivables and the reputation of the creditors.

Barter. If your creditor appears to have trouble paying you but can provide a product or service you need, take that in exchange for the amount owed.

Sue. As a last resort, take your customer to court and sue to collect the amount owed plus interest, court costs, and damages, if any.

CASH INVESTMENTS

Envy the business that has a cash surplus. Being cash-rich doesn't solve all your problems, but it is sure a lot better than being cash-poor. It is worth mentioning that good cash-management practices can help move a business from being cash-poor to cash-rich. When interest rates stand at 15 percent or more, large increases in revenue are possible through the investment of surplus funds. Let's assume your checking account averaged $10,000 for the year. If this was invested at 15 percent rather than being left in your checking account you would gain $1,500 per year. If you delayed paying your bills so your bank account could swell to $20,000, you would have pocketed another $1,500. If you can speed up collections, in essence you're increasing your bank balance—and your opportunity to gain.

Take the following cash-management self-assessment test. If you answer no to any of the following questions, you may be losing potential profit:

1. Does your business have a money-fund account?
2. Do you wait until the due date to pay your bills unless there is a cash discount?
3. Do you take favorable cash discounts when available?
4. Are you familiar with the options available to businesses for investment of surplus cash?
5. Do you know the annual interest you could earn on the average balance in your checking account?
6. Does your business have an account with a brokerage firm for investing in stocks and bonds?
7. Do you have a savings account in your bank so that very short-term funds can draw interest?

Investing excess cash is neither a complex nor a time-consuming task. If your business has large amounts of money, you may wish to engage a professional money manager to optimize your investment potential. However, even with small amounts of funds, investment income of several hundred or thousand dollars can be earned that might otherwise be lost.

Businesses need to develop an investment philosophy similar to the type used by an individual. Businesses may wish to make conservative investments, or riskier ones that generate higher revenues, or a combination of the two. This guidance needs to be given to the money manager *prior* to his investing of your funds.

Conservative investments a company can use include:

- Savings accounts in banks.
- Certificates of deposit.
- Money funds.
- Repurchase agreements at banks.
- Treasury bills.
- High-grade short-term bonds.

Riskier but higher-yield investments include:

- Long-term corporate bonds.
- Stocks.
- Real estate.
- Raw land.
- Other businesses.

Most businesses will experience cash-flow problems periodically. Some experience them continuously, usually because their owners have neglected to manage their business or cash properly. Solutions are available for the short-term cash problem, but possibly only a restructuring of the business can help in the long term.

Let's examine some of the conditions that can cause businesses to experience short-term difficulties:

- Expenditure for a capital purchase.
- Downturn in the economy that causes delays in both sales and collections.
- Purchase of large amounts of inventory to gain quantity discount prices.
- Advance cash payments to receive cash-payment discounts.
- Short-term investments that cannot be returned to cash for a predetermined period, such as a 90-day certificate of deposit in a bank, which carries a penalty if redeemed early.

The test of a good cash manager is the ease with which he can survive a cash crisis. The experienced manager pulls from his bag of tricks the necessary trump cards to meet the challenge. The poor cash manager spends his time on the phone explaining to creditors that it will only be a few more days until the bills are paid.

Let's review the cash manager's options for solving a cash-flow crisis:

Stretching payments selectively. Some businesses are more lenient than others on payments. The cash manager needs to find the lenient businesses and delay payments to them. Many times a phone call asking for an extra few days or weeks is accepted, and your business then lives on the other business's money.

Improve collections selectively. Some customers may be willing to pay early, knowing a business is experiencing a cash-flow problem. Nothing ventured, nothing gained.

Borrow from owners and/or key employees. People with a vested interest in the business may be willing to make short- or long-term loans to the business. These can and should be interest-bearing loans.

Short-term bank loans. Lines of credit from banks should be secured in advance so that when short-term loans are needed they are available.

Offer marketing bonuses. Offer special bonuses to the marketing force if it can sell large quantities of product on a cash basis within the needed time.

Special-purchase discounts. Offer some or all customers special discounts if they buy large quantities of product on a cash basis within the needed period.

Employee layoff (temporary or permanent). Payroll costs can be reduced by laying off people for short periods. However, note that firing people may, in fact, cause a short-term cash strain if it is necessary to pay severance or reimburse for benefits such as vacation or sick days. Layoffs can also increase your unemployment tax payments.

CASH FLOW CONSIDERATIONS

Mailbox watchers can become frustrated when expected revenue is delayed. The delays can seem endless, and prodding phone calls may bring nothing more than repeated promises to pay within a few days. Living continuously with a cash crisis is a poor way to conduct business. The alternative is to manage cash.

The tools that a business should consider in developing a cash management program are:

- *Cash analysis.* The assignment of people, methods, tools, and techniques needed to track the receipt and use of cash in the business.
- *Methods to improve cash flow.* Good cash flow doesn't just happen, it is a result of good people using good cash-management techniques. Proper use of these procedures should improve cash flow.
- *Methods of using cash.* Idle cash wastes business resources just as idle employees waste resources. Businesses should put idle cash to work.

CHAPTER HIGHLIGHT

Bills are paid with cash, not profits. Managing cash flow is an essential part of business survival.

CASH-MANAGEMENT QUESTIONS

If you are concerned about your cash-management procedures, you should ask your accountant:

QUESTION: How much cash should I have on hand to run my business?

CONSIDERATIONS: The amount of cash you need to run a business depends on your short-term requirements to pay bills, plus cash for any capital purchases you may be making in the near future. This amount of money will vary from week to week and month to month. In order to determine the exact amount of cash you need, perform a cash-flow analysis on your business.

QUESTION: Should I maintain available cash in both a checking and a savings account?

CONSIDERATIONS: Cash management is a method of ensuring that you have cash when you need it. Its only requirement is that money be available when necessary. This generally implies that available cash will be maintained in an investment that enables you to convert it into cash quickly, whether in a bank or certificate of deposit (CD) is up to you and your risk philosophy.

QUESTION: How can I determine my short-term cash needs?

CONSIDERATIONS: History is a good indicator of your future cash needs. Most of your bills will continue to come due during certain weeks of the month and months of the year. You should plot your major bills—tax bills, loan repayments, rent—throughout the year. Next, estimate the average weekly expenditures for inventory, payroll, and so forth. The combination of the two totals will give you an idea of the amount of cash you will need each week.

QUESTION: How can I estimate my expected revenue?

CONSIDERATIONS: Estimating cash revenue is similar to estimating cash needs. Any large-income items, such as contract payments, should be individually identified. After excluding these extraordinary items, history should be the basis of determining average weekly or monthly cash revenue.

QUESTION: What type of statements should I prepare for a projected cash-flow analysis?

CONSIDERATIONS: The form or type of statement is unimportant, as long as you can show on a daily, weekly, or monthly basis (whatever is most relevant to your business) the expected cash income and the cash needs for the same period. The statement should show four pieces of information for each period:

- Expected revenue.
- Cash needs.
- Overage or underage for the period.
- Accumulated overage or underage for the period covered on the statement.

A business should not expect to have identical cash income and outflow for every period throughout the year. Thus, it is necessary to show both the overage and underage for a period and the accumulated overage and underage. This shows both the short-term and long-term cash position of the business.

QUESTION: Who should prepare the cash flow analysis?

CONSIDERATIONS: The individual responsible for paying the business's bills should be given responsibility for managing cash. It is this person's responsibility to ensure that sufficient funds are available to keep the business solvent.

QUESTION: How do I know whether my projection is realistic?

CONSIDERATIONS: Projections are planning tools. There is no guarantee your estimates will be accurate, regardless of the amount of time and effort you put into them. What you must do is continually monitor actual conditions against the projections. If conditions change, you must change your estimates accordingly. Since your cash-management program is based on your projections, you will need to take action if reality varies significantly from them. If income exceeds expectations and expenditures stay the same, you need to change your investment strategy. If revenue stays the same but expenses increase, you will need to raise cash to maintan the solvency of your business. These trends need to be closely monitored and the necessary action taken.

QUESTION: If my cash flow is positive, does that mean my business is making a profit?
CONSIDERATIONS: An increase in the amount of available cash does *not* necessarily mean your business is making a profit. Cash can be generated by consuming assets. For example, as you depreciate your capital assets, the amount of available cash should increase, as it will when you begin to deplete your inventory. On the other hand, reduction in cash does not necessarily mean you are losing money. If you are buying more assets or inventory, your cash position can be worsening but your business may still be showing a healthy profit as cash is put into the acquisition of other assets. This is why it is important to measure your profitability and monitor your cash position.
QUESTION: For what periods should I develop a cash-flow analysis?
CONSIDERATIONS: Businesses should develop both long-term and short-term analyses. The long-term cash-flow analysis should be for a year; a shorter-term analysis should be for a three-month period. A new analysis should be developed at the end of the three-month period.

METHODS TO IMPROVE CASH FLOW

If you anticipate cash shortages, you should ask your accountant:

QUESTION: Should my business have cash shortages throughout the year?
CONSIDERATIONS: Most businesses have variations in their cash flow. In some periods they will have surplus cash, while in other periods they will have shortages. What is bad is to be surprised by a cash shortage. Good cash management can anticipate and take steps to deal with periods of low cash availability.
QUESTION: What can I do in my business to maintain a good credit rating during periods of low cash availability?

CONSIDERATIONS: Many suggestions for improving your cash flow have been outlined in this chapter. The methods cover both techniques for increasing revenue and reducing expenditures. During the periods in which you anticipate a cash shortage, you should determine which of those methods you intend to use and in which order. For example, you may decide you do not want to pressure your customers for cash and would rather delay paying your bills. What is important is that you have a strategy to follow, so you know exactly what you will do when the shortage occurs.

QUESTION: During periods of short cash wouldn't it be better to borrow funds than risk upsetting customers or vendors?

CONSIDERATIONS: Borrowing incurs an additional interest expense for your business, while other methods of management may not. For example, delaying payment of some bills may shift the burden of finding additional funds to your vendors. However, you will have to weigh the impact these alternate methods may have on receiving favorable treatment from your customers or vendors in the future. If you believe the "low-cost" methods of surviving cash crises have significant negative side effects, it may be worth the cost of borrowing.

QUESTION: Wouldn't it be better to keep a large cash reserve than periodically to experience cash-flow problems?

CONSIDERATIONS: Cash is a resource of your business. If it's idle for long periods of time, you are losing the income derived from that resource, just as you would lose money by having extra employees sit around when there is a need for their services. A better policy is to develop a realistic cash management program to minimize your periods of cash shortage and maximize the value you receive from the cash in your business.

METHODS OF USING CASH

If you have available cash in your business, you might ask your accountant:

QUESTION: Where should I invest my surplus cash funds?

CONSIDERATIONS: Your accountant is not an investment counselor. He does, however, know where other businesses are investing their surplus funds. Look to your accountant for advice as to *where* you should invest your surplus funds, not the specific investment itself. The final investment choice is yours, but you should get the best professional investment advice you can before you make your decision. If you have large amounts of cash to invest, you might consider obtaining the advice of an investment counselor.

QUESTION: What type of return on investment is realistic to expect?

CONSIDERATIONS: The return you get on your investment depends on the amount of risk you want to take. Investing in insured accounts with a bank or in treasury bills is the safest of all investments but produces the lowest return. As the risk of the investment increases, so does the potential return. Your decision is: how much risk do you want to take?

QUESTION: Why would my business want to spend time and effort on investing cash resources when our expertise is in another field?

CONSIDERATIONS: Your long-range investment objective should be to build your own business. That is what you know and that is what you do best. However, you need some cash reserves for safety, and you will have periods of cash surpluses. These cash reserves provide an opportunity to increase the profitability of your business and it would be poor management not to capitalize upon that opportunity.

QUESTION: Will I be required to pay taxes on investment income in addition to those I must pay on the income from my normal business operations?

CONSIDERATIONS: Your investment income will be taxed at the same rate as income from normal operations unless you put your money into tax-exempt investments. Some municipalities tax businesses on their assets, and certain investments, such as stocks, may be considered assets and therefore be subject to a special tax. Investigate the tax considerations prior to selecting your investment.

CHAPTER 12

Controlling Record Keeping

THE mightiest of systems can crumble when its basic records are inaccurate. Systems people have coined a phrase that explains poor record keeping: "GIGO," which means "garbage in—garbage out." A system is no better than the accuracy of its records.

The objective of any record-keeping system is to process correct, complete, and authorized transactions and the system should be designed to do so. Record-keeping policies, procedures, and controls will determine the integrity of processing.

Businesses must establish record-keeping systems, acquire the resources necessary to operate those systems, and control them to ensure the validity of processing.

OFFICE POLICIES AND PROCEDURES

Offices operate in accordance with management's policies, written or unwritten. The lack of a policy is in itself a policy. For example, if there is no policy on how long one can take for lunch then employees assume they are permitted a reasonable and proper lunch period—probably of one hour or longer.

Many policies in a small business are informal, established by what the boss does and says as opposed to what is actually written down. The staff's coffee break may continue until the boss gets up and goes back to work. Employees know that the coffee-break policy is to continue relaxing until the boss leaves.

Offices generally function better when policies and procedures are documented and understood by both management and employees. Having this information makes it easier for the employee to understand and comply with the desires of management.

The types of policies that businesses should establish include:

- Working hours.
- Sickness call-in and payment.
- Methods for performing record keeping.
- Timeliness of record keeping.
- Expected reliability of record keeping.
- Responsibility for authorizing actions.
- Authority for dealing with customers, vendors, and contractors.
- Job responsibilities.
- Vacation and holiday alternatives.

WHAT ARE CONTROLS?

Controls are measures initiated by management which ensure that events happen in accordance with the intent of management. The objective of control is to make things work the right way and to detect and correct problems, should they occur. The basis for control is prevention or detection of problems. If businesses do not have problems, they do not need controls. In other words, in a perfect environment controls are unnecessary.

Controls should be cost-effective: if you are concerned about employees taking Scotch tape home, it is not cost-effective to buy a $2,000 safe in which to store twelve rolls of $1.29 Scotch tape. The savings achieved by having effective controls should exceed the cost of the control.

Follow these steps in designing your controls:

Step 1. Identify potential problems. The basis for control is to identify all of the problems that may need resolution or clarification.

Step 2. Determine the magnitude of problems. If the problem is minimal, there may be no need for control. If it is determined to be of major importance, such as mispricing customer invoices that results in a loss of revenue of $25,000 per year or more, it would be worth controlling.

Step 3. Determine how much loss is acceptable. Controls will not necessarily assure perfect results. The owner needs to judge how accurate processing must be in different areas. For example, the owner may decide that invoices off by a dollar or two are acceptable, but payroll checks must be accurate to the penny.

Step 4. Establish control objective. After making a judgment on the required degree of accuracy, a business person must establish a realistic specific control objective, such as reducing billing errors to plus or minus $1 per salesperson per shift.

Step 5. Select the control. Controls are selected to meet the control objectives.

CONTROLLING AUTHORIZATION OF EVENTS

The business needs to ensure that events occur in accordance with the intent of management. Employees can obligate a business in the following ways:

- Agree to sell product at a given price.
- Agree to perform certain services for a customer.
- Agree to buy product from a vendor.

Management needs to identify each type of transaction in which the business engages. It should then determine who is responsible for purchasing that product or service, for example, who in the company can order office supplies or who can buy inventory, and then ensure that those are the only individuals who perform that function.

RECORDING BUSINESS TRANSACTIONS

Transactions should be recorded when they occur since that is the time the employee is most familiar with them and has the highest probability of recording them correctly. Also, a second individual may be involved who can help confirm the accuracy of the transaction and recording.

Most errors made in record-keeping systems occur at the point of recording the transaction. The more common type of errors include:

- Wrong customer name or number.
- Wrong address.
- Wrong date.
- Wrong amounts.
- Wrong form.

The recording method will vary with the type of business you're in. The goal should be to conduct the financial recording as a by-product of the transaction. For example, a cash register records a transaction at the time funds are accepted and change is made.

The golden rules of recording are discussed below.

Keep it simple. If the method of recording a transaction is complex, people are going to foul it up.

Use self-explanatory collection forms (or equivalent). The recording media should indicate what information is expected. For example, if the date is wanted, space should be allocated on the recording media to indicate the date.

Indicate responsibility. An indication should be made of who recorded the transaction, for two reasons: to pinpoint accountability; and to identify the individual to whom questions can be addressed.

Use self-checking information. The form should provide, wherever practical, information that helps to verify the correctness of the recorded data or to detect a potential problem. For example, on an order the entry may ask for both the item number and the description. If there is an inconsistency between the two it would call attention to a discrepancy.

Limit the number of people who record. As a general rule, the fewer people record financial transactions, the better the system will function.

Provide independent controls. Owners should establish controls external to the actual recording operation to verify the recordings. For example, an employee has to balance the cash drawer to the cash register total.

ESTABLISHING CONTROLS OVER TRANSACTIONS

Businesses should establish minimal levels of control to provide a high probability that transactions are recorded accurately and completely. Listed below are some controls applicable to the chief resources of an organization:

Personnel

- Use of timeclocks or other methods to record start and stop times.
- Maintain files on employee errors (for use in firing).
- Maintain log of absences and vacation days.

Cash Receipts

- Use cash registers or other automated devices to record sales.

- Give the customer a receipt as a means of verifying the accuracy of price(s) charged.
- Use one clerk to sell a product and another to receive funds for the sale.
- Use a different cash drawer for each employee.
- Make employees reconcile receipts to recorded sales.

Inventory

- Record inventory at selling price and reconcile to sales.
- Take regular physical inventories.
- Make individuals accountable for inventory under their control.
- Record inventory items sold and reconcile to on-hand inventory.

Sales

- Reconcile supplies to sales if practical; for example, in food stores reconcile cups used to soft drinks sold and in movie theaters compare the ratio of popcorn sold to theater attendees.
- Compare value of inventory used to sales.
- Calculate gross profit and investigate variations from norm.

Purchases

- Have all items delivered to a person other than the one who ordered them.
- Match the receiving document to the purchase order prior to payment.
- Have only one receiving document to match to the invoice to avoid paying duplicate invoices.

EMPLOYEE THEFT

Statistics have shown that you will lose more resources to your employees than to outside parties. You should recognize this as your major threat and establish controls to reduce it. Also, controls that are effective against employee theft are normally effective against thefts by outside parties.

Let's look at some of the ways employees can circumvent recording transactions so they can pocket your resources. An employee can:

- Sell a product but fail to record it.
- Buy a product for personal use, but pay for it with business funds.
- Give a friend merchandise but not charge them, or charge them less than the normal price.
- Use your equipment, supplies, and resources for personal use.
- Do work for other businesses on your time.
- Sell or do work for your customers personally so that the employee gains and not you.

Never underestimate the ingenuity of your employees. One of the sad facts of life is that often the most trusted employees are the ones who embezzle. The business person has an obligation to make it as difficult as possible for employees to defraud the business.

RECORD-KEEPING CONSIDERATIONS

In recording and controlling usiness transactions, the owner should consider:

- *Policies and procedures.* The rules employees are to follow in maintaining and controlling records.
- *Record-keeping system.* The steps that employees are to follow in recording the results of transactions.

- *Cost-effectiveness.* The economics of the record-keeping function.
- *Controls.* The measures that ensure the accuracy, completeness, and authorization of recorded transactions.
- *Integrity.* The correctness of the record-keeping totals.

CHAPTER HIGHLIGHT

Good controls help increase profits through prevention and detection of improper practices and help prevent losses owing to carelessness.

QUESTIONS ABOUT POLICIES AND PROCEDURES

If you are uncertain of the adequacy of your office procedures, you might ask your accountant:

QUESTION: Are my office policies and procedures reasonable and complete?
CONSIDERATIONS: Accountants work in many different offices and gain an appreciation of the commonly accepted office policies and procedures. They can provide you with an assessment of yours compared to those of similar organizations in your community.
QUESTION: Are my policies and procedures in compliance with government regulations?
CONSIDERATIONS: Generally, office policies and procedures are not covered by regulations, but it may be helpful to have your accountant review them to be sure.

RECORD-KEEPING QUESTIONS

Questions you might ask your accountant regarding the adequacy of your record-keeping methods are:

QUESTION: Does my system collect sufficient information on cash receipts to substantiate income?

CONSIDERATIONS: The two concerns are tax and theft. Good control procedures recommend the recording of receipts at the time of sale, using a process such as cash-register tapes or prenumbered sales tickets that will detect missing receipts. The information collected should include date, customer, product, quantity, price, tax, shipping charges (if any), and salesperson.

QUESTION: Do the cash-disbursement records substantiate the accuracy and completeness of payments?

CONSIDERATIONS: The two main concerns are tax and duplicate payments. Good control procedures demand a system of approval on expenditures prior to the payment. Control should be established at the point of approval, for example using a prenumbered document. The actual cash disbursement should reference that control number to avoid duplicate payments. The information collected should include date, vendor, product or service acquired, quantity, price, and proof of receipt.

QUESTION: Do the payroll records contain sufficient data to substantiate employee salaries and taxes withheld and owed?

CONSIDERATIONS: Good practice and some regulations require you to keep records on employee hours of work and absences (state causes). It is also good practice to have the employee countersign the record of hours to substantiate its correctness.

QUESTION: Should all the cash receipts be deposited intact daily in the bank?

CONSIDERATIONS: According to good business practice, cash receipts should be identified in the records and deposited intact in the bank so the recording of income can be substantiated.

QUESTION: Should a petty-cash fund be established for small expenditures?
CONSIDERATIONS: A special fund should be available to make small purchases. This eliminates the temptation to use cash receipts for this purpose.
QUESTION: Should all expenditures be paid for by check?
CONSIDERATIONS: According to good business practice, checks should be used to pay for all expenditures because they then provide a formal record of the transaction.
QUESTION: Should a bank account be established for the exclusive use of the business?
CONSIDERATIONS: It is poor business practice to intermingle personal and business funds. Upon starting a business, a bank account(s) should be established to deposit all receipts and pay all bills.
QUESTION: Should the name of the individual who recorded the transaction be associated with the record so the individual can be held accountable?
CONSIDERATIONS: Yes.
QUESTION: How can I assess the adequacy of my controls?
CONSIDERATIONS: Your accountant can provide you with a control checklist, or you can write to the American Institute of CPAs, 1211 Avenue of the Americas, New York, NY 10036 for a list of their current manuals, books, audit guides, and training courses on small-business-system controls.

COST-EFFECTIVENESS QUESTIONS

If you are concerned about the cost of your record-keeping system, you should ask your accountant:

QUESTION: Am I recording too much information for revenue transactions?
CONSIDERATIONS: If information is being recorded that is not used or required, funds are being spent needlessly.

QUESTION: Am I recording too much information for my cash disbursements?

CONSIDERATIONS: Recording information that is not needed to substantiate disbursements is an unnecessary expenditure of time.

QUESTION: Could my record keeping be performed using a more cost-effective method?

CONSIDERATIONS: You should give your accountant the opportunity to recommend alternate methods for recording information. These alternate methods may include computers, service bureaus, pegboard systems, or others.

QUESTION: Am I recording duplicate information unnecessarily?

CONSIDERATIONS: Many systems record the same information more than once. If this is not necessary to facilitate answering questions or for some other purpose it should be eliminated.

QUESTION: Would other methods of record keeping enable me to locate needed information more quickly?

CONSIDERATIONS: If your business is having problems locating information fast enough, your system can be redesigned to alleviate that problem. Time spent searching for information is wasted. In addition, if it is difficult to obtain information, you might not look for it, and thus be unaware of situations in which you are losing money. For example, a customer's account may be three months overdue and yet your business still gives that customer more credit because your system does not advise you of problems fast enough.

QUESTION: Is the recording being done in the most effective way?

CONSIDERATIONS: If the wrong person is doing the recording, it may require extra time, or use the time of people whose skills would be better used elsewhere. It is good practice to have the person who performs a task, such as making a sale, record all of the needed information as a corollary of performing that event.

CONTROL QUESTIONS

If you feel controls are inadequate, you should ask your accountant:

QUESTION: How difficult would it be for one of my employees to steal revenue?
CONSIDERATIONS: Weak controls encourage theft. Your accountant should be able to evaluate your cash-receipts controls and provide an opinion as to their inadequacy.
QUESTION: Are the controls over my payroll system adequate to prevent employees from being paid for time they do not work?
CONSIDERATIONS: Controls on recording time on the job can be reviewed by your accountant so he can make a judgment as to whether it is possible for employees to report as working hours time when they did not work.
QUESTION: Are controls over orders sufficient to make sure my business bills for all products we ship?
CONSIDERATIONS: One way a business can lose large amounts of money is to ship products and then not prepare, or lose, the necessary paperwork so the customer is not billed for that work. An effective control is to prepare a two-part invoice prior to shipping. The first copy is the control to ensure billing, while the second copy (the shipping document) controls shipping, since no product can be sent without it.
QUESTION: Are controls over purchases sufficient to ensure receipt of all merchandise paid for?
CONSIDERATIONS: Many businesses use receiving reports to substantiate that purchased items have been received. Receiving is done by someone independent of the person who writes out the purchase order. The receiving clerk records whatever is actually received on the receiving reports, which are matched to the purchase orders. Payments are made only when a match occurs. Without this or a similar control, you may be paying for merchandise not received or receiving merchandise other than what you ordered.

QUESTION: Are my controls good enough to prevent loss of cash receipts?

CONSIDERATIONS: Cash receipts should be recorded immediately. Whoever receives the cash should create a control total and then separate the cash from the cash records. Unless control is established at the point of receipt, the probability exists that funds can be lost or embezzled.

QUESTION: When cash receipts are in the form of checks, are they immediately restrictively endorsed to ensure they cannot be cashed if stolen?

CONSIDERATIONS: Most banks provide businesses with a stamp to restrictively endorse checks. Businesses large enough to have a mail room or who assign someone to open mail normally have that individual restrictively endorse each check.

QUESTION: Are my controls over inventory adequate for a timely detection of missing inventory?

CONSIDERATIONS: Inventory can be lost through incorrect shipment and theft. Businesses can usually deal with a control problem if they know the problem exists. If inventory losses can be detected only as a result of an annual inventory, the business may be losing substantial amounts during the year and not know it. A good control practice is to take inventory quarterly and then estimate what sales should be on the basis of inventory usage. If actual sales are less than inventory usage there is probably lost inventory. At that point additional inventory controls, such as spot checking the accuracy of shipments and locking up inventory may be warranted.

QUESTION: Should someone other than the individual who signs checks reconcile the bank statement?

CONSIDERATIONS: Yes. Except for in very small businesses, the bank account should be reconciled by someone other than the individual who signs the checks. This helps ensure the integrity of the checking account and provides one more control over the propriety of expenditures.

QUESTION: Do my business controls ensure that my employees cannot use business resources for their personal gain?

CONSIDERATIONS: If your business can make money using your resources, so can your employees. Procedures should be established to ensure that employees can only use the resources of your business for authorized purposes. Since most abuses occur when employees are alone, it's good practice not to let one employee work alone.

QUESTION: Are my customers and customer records protected so that my employees cannot take away my business?

CONSIDERATIONS: While you may not have the right to deny your employees' taking your customers' business from you, be alert to that possibility and install controls wherever possible to limit the probability. Controls include safeguarding customer name-and-address lists and notifying customers, when key employees become competitors, that these former employees are no longer working for you, so that your customers will not think they are still purchasing from you.

QUESTION: Are my negotiable instruments and other accountable documents adequately controlled?

CONSIDERATIONS: Documents that have value, such as checks, should be stored in a locked cabinet so they cannot be misused.

QUESTION: Does my system of controls adequately protect my business against losses?

CONSIDERATIONS: Controls should provide a check on the accuracy and completeness of operations. Verifying totals independent of operations—such as reconciling bank statements to cash receipts and disbursement journals—provides this check. The independent control should be performed by a person other than the one who performs the operation being checked. For example, the person who writes checks should not reconcile the bank statement (except, of course, when the owner writes the checks).

QUESTION: Should I be able to support all of my financial totals with the underlying transactions?

CONSIDERATIONS: All financial totals should be supportable. The owners should know how each total is supported and where the supporting documentation is filed.

QUESTIONS ABOUT INTEGRITY

If you are concerned about the integrity of your financial totals, you should ask your accountant:

QUESTION: Do the balances in my detailed accounts-receivable records add up to the total amount on my invoice copies?
CONSIDERATIONS: Periodically, the accounts-receivable records should be totaled to verify that they support the amount due as recorded on customers' invoices. Generally this should be done monthly, unless balancing problems occur, in which case weekly reconciliations are advisable. If the detailed records do not balance with the control totals, the correct recording of each transaction should be verified during the reconciliation.

QUESTION: Does my on-hand inventory equal the book inventory?
CONSIDERATIONS: You should take a physical inventory periodically to verify that your on-hand count equals the book inventory. You may have to make some adjustments in the reconciliation process; if you are uncertain as to how to do so your accountant can help you. Quarterly inventory counts are recommended unless significant differences are detected, in which case monthly counts may be advisable.

QUESTION: Does your cash on hand reconcile with the book cash balance?
CONSIDERATIONS: Businesses should develop simple accounting proofs for their cash. Essentially, these are the same as those used to balance a checkbook: begin with last month's cash balance, add receipts, and subtract expenditures. The new book balance should reconcile to the actual cash balance.

Section IV

ANALYZING OPERATIONS

One of the reasons to maintain accounting records is to provide sufficient information to enable management to analyze operations and take corrective action wherever operating can be improved.

CHAPTER 13

Constructing Financial Statements

THE bottom line indicates the level of profitability of a business, but it doesn't tell the whole story. Paraphrasing an old adage, one might say, "Accounting doesn't lie, but liars can manipulate accounting." There are literally a thousand ways to compute the bottom line, so if you don't read the whole story you won't know the meaning of the conclusions.

Tales still circulate in big corporations about how fifty years ago the president would visit the accounting department at year end and tell them how much profit he wanted that year. It was then up to the accountants to manipulate the records so the company achieved it. Accounting, you see, is not an exact science but, rather, a series of rules that can be applied many ways.

INTERPRETING FINANCIAL STATEMENTS

Let's state the facts about what to expect when you see a financial statement. The dollars shown on the financial statement are real dollars. The accounts are real accounts. The totals are normally computed correctly, and the records are usually maintained in accordance with generally accepted accounting procedures. This would lead the uninitiated to believe that two accountants preparing financial statements for the same business would produce the same statements. False. You and your accountant have flexibility in preparing financial statements. Let's examine a statement for the "Hypothetical Corporation" prepared by two different accountants.

In example A, the Hypothetical Corporation shows a profit on the statement of income and expense (see Figure 8). The bottom line is positive, and the owners should feel good about the results of operations for the year. When we look at example B, however, it shows that the business *lost* money for the year. But the statements cover the same business; they show the same amount of sales. All operations were performed the same way—except that the accountants made some different accounting decisions when they prepared the financial statements.

Let's look at what the accountants did differently in the two examples to come out with a profit in example A and a loss in example B:

- In example A the accountant used straight-line depreciation of 10 percent, which results in a deduction from sales of $10,000. In example B the accountant used double-declining-balance depreciation and was able to deduct $20,000 from profit.
- In example B the accountant recommended that the business buy next year's expendable supplies early, so it could write off another $1,000 of expenses. In example A they waited until next year to buy the supplies.
- In example B the accountant recommended writing off $2,000 of accounts receivable as bad debts, while in example A the business decided to wait longer to determine whether the debts were really bad.
- Hypothetical Corporation has been paying its manager a $5,000 bonus on January 1, but for this year the

accountant in example B recommended it be paid on December 31 so the business would gain another $5,000 deduction.

Figure 8

HYPOTHETICAL COMPANY STATEMENT OF INCOME AND EXPENSE

EXAMPLE A

SALES		$120,000
Less: cost of sales		
Inventory	$40,000	
Depreciation	10,000	
Marketing salary and expenses	30,000	80,000
GROSS PROFIT		$ 40,000
Less: administrative expenses		
Administrative salaries	$20,000	
Expenses	5,000	
Bad debt write-off	—	
Management bonus	—	25,000
NET PROFIT		$ 15,000

EXAMPLE B

SALES		$120,000
Less: cost of sales		
Inventory	$40,000	
Depreciation	20,000	
Marketing salary and expenses	30,000	90,000
GROSS PROFIT		$30,000
Less: administrative expenses		
Administrative salaries	$20,000	
Expenses	6,000	
Bad debt write-off	2,000	
Management bonus	5,000	33,000
NET PROFIT		($ 3,000)

The net result of these accounting changes is the difference between a $15,000 profit and a $3,000 loss, or a shift of $18,000. In example A the business has to pay taxes on its profit, while in example B the business has lost money and pays no tax. (This is discussed in more detail in the chapter on income taxes.) The point is that the business can legitimately affect the amount of profit or loss it will incur in any one year.

FINANCIAL DISCLOSURE

The government and professional accounting associations such as the American Institute of Certified Public Accountants and the Canadian Institute of Chartered Accountants specify the format and content of financial statements. Businesses are expected to comply with these generally accepted accounting procedures. Certified accountants understand and can apply these accounting principles to your business.

We just saw how businesses could legitimately change the amount of profit or loss reported in a given year. These methods are well known to accountants and investors. But it is important that the general public also understands the methods used in preparing statements. According to generally accepted procedures, these facts must be disclosed in the footnotes of your financial statements.

In our case of the Hypothetical Corporation we show that in example B the accountants used an accelerated depreciation method, which significantly reduced profits. This is the type of information that needs to be disclosed in your financial statements or the statements might be misleading to investors. For example, we saw that the Hypothetical Corporation under one set of accounting conditions made $15,000 profit but under another set of conditions lost $3,000. If the investor was unaware of the accounting methods used, he might feel after reading the example A statement that the company was far better managed than after reading the B statement.

Some of the information that should be disclosed in financial statements includes:

- Percent of the business owned by officers and members of the board of directors.
- Variations from generally accepted accounting procedures.
- Changes in accounting methods, such as going from an inventory method, which charged the most recent cost of purchases to sales (last in, first out—or LIFO), to a method which charged the oldest cost of purchases and inventory to sales (first in, first out—or FIFO).
- Accelerated-depreciation methods.
- Special one-time write-offs, resulting in an unusual expenditure or income.
- Sale of major assets.

WHO PREPARES FINANCIAL STATEMENTS?

Financial statements can be prepared by a qualified individual in your business or by your accountant. In firms with computers, the financial statement may be prepared by the computer. As in most other aspects of business, the financial statements should be prepared by the individual who can do it most knowledgeably and most economically.

Even when the business prepares the financial statements, the role of an independent accountant is important. He is versed in generally accepted accounting procedures and can review the statements to ensure their compliance with those regulations. In addition, the accountant can determine what type of information needs to be disclosed on the financial statements. In businesses without a qualified staff accountant, the independent accountant may also prepare the financial statements.

TYPES OF FINANCIAL STATEMENTS

The complete financial statement tells the story of what the business and the accountant have done. Unfortunately, many people focus on the bottom line and don't take the time and effort to read the whole, which may not be as exciting but is as important in interpreting the meaning of the statement.

Businesses should prepare three kinds of financial statements:

- *Balance sheet.* The balance sheet shows the value of the assets, the amount of debt, and the owner's equity in the business as of a particular date. In order to prepare the balance sheet, one must determine the ending financial balances (such as the actual amount of inventory on hand, the cash in the bank, and the profit or loss that the business has incurred up to that date). Thus, the balance sheet cannot be prepared independent of the statement of income and ex-

penses. The balance sheet is important to investors and banks because it is helpful in identifying the business's ability to pay its debts and in determining an approximate value of the business.
- *Statement of income and expenses.* This statement shows all of the revenue and all of the expenses. The difference between the two is the business's profit or loss.
- *Source and application of funds.* This statement shows where cash has come from and where it has gone. All revenue is not cash because many of your sales may be made on credit and thus become receivables, and all of your expenses are not paid for with cash; for example, depreciation is an expense for the use of an asset paid for with cash in earlier years. In addition, your business may make expenditures that cannot be immediately or fully deducted from revenue on your statement of income and expense. An example might be the incorporation expenses or franchise fees, which must be amortized over a period of years.

FREQUENCY OF STATEMENTS

As a rule businesses prepare a full complement of financial statements at the end of their business year, when they are required to for tax reasons (and reports to stockholders, if the business is a corporation). These are normally the formal statements of the business and the statements given to potential investors or banks.

Most businesses also prepare financial statements quarterly. The major corporations commonly do this, sending copies to their stockholders. Smaller businesses may choose not to prepare financial statements as frequently. Many franchisers require their franchisees to prepare monthly statements. They have learned that this focuses the franchisee's attention on financial matters. The franchisers also know that businesses that closely watch their financial statements and make adjustments according to actual results tend to be more successful than those who are not so attentive. The franchisers provide special forms so the franchisees can prepare and list all of the necessary financial information. Franchisers are particularly concerned with ratios as a measure of how well the business is being run. All small businesses could learn from franchises and consider following the practice of issuing monthly financial statements.

Some of the more valuable ratios used to analyze operations include:

- *Inventory turnover.* The number of times your business sells its average inventory value per year. This tells how effectively your business utilizes inventory (i.e., you may have too much inventory if your ratio is too low for your industry).
- *Administrative expenses as a percent of sales.* Indicates how efficiently you administer your business.
- *Number of stockouts to number of items sold.* Too many stockouts may indicate your inventory is too low.
- *Sales per employee.* Low sales under the norm for your industry may indicate you have too many employees.
- *Average collection days.* The average number of days to collect receivables indicates the effectiveness of your collection procedures.

The reasons for using regular financial statements are:

- To monitor the adequacy of the inventory on hand.
- To monitor the collection of receivables (while a special statement was not identified for receivables, many businesses prepare an "aging" statement showing receivables outstanding for over thirty days).
- To show bottom-line profitability.

- To report cost of sales to determine whether or not prices should be increased or decreased.
- To show administrative expenses as a percent of sales to determine how well these expenses are being managed.

It may not be necessary to put the same time and effort that goes into preparing annual financial statements into quarterly or monthly statements. It is probably unnecessary to count inventory physically, although many businesses do so on a monthly basis, or to make many of the adjustments necessary at year end, such as writing off bad debts more than once a year.

Occasionally businesses—normally those in financial difficulty—find it necessary to prepare financial statements more frequently than once a month in order to closely monitor cash flow and profitability. These, however, are unusual situations, and monthly statements should suffice for most businesses.

IS AN AUDIT NECESSARY?

An audit is an independent evaluation of the financial statements. An audit does not attempt to provide assurance that the financial statements are correct, but only that they are reasonable. While reasonableness is not defined by law, it is generally accepted to mean that the stated financial balances are within 5 percent of the correct balance. The audit also determines whether the financial statements were prepared in accordance with generally accepted accounting procedures and on a basis consistent with previous years.

Publicly held companies listed on stock exchanges are required to have their statements audited by independent accountants. Their statements carry an opinion by the independent accountant of the reasonableness of the statements. If you review the annual reports of publicly held companies, you will note a short statement by the business's accounting firm included within the financial statements. If the accounting firm feels there is something unusual about the financial statements, they will say so in their opinion. This is referred to as a *qualified opinion*.

A small business may desire to have its financial statements audited because:

- It may be necessary in order to obtain a bank loan.
- It may be required in order to sell stock.
- One or more of the owners may request it.

The independent accountant (CPA or CA) is required to follow a standard method of auditing prescribed by their professional accounting association if a client wants his statements certified.

Most small businesses do not need audited statements. A letter from the accountant accompanying the financial statement is sufficient for most banks or investors. This transmittal letter explains what the accountant did in preparing and examining the financial data and provides a basis for third parties such as banks to accept the financial statements as reasonable.

FINANCIAL-STATEMENT CONSIDERATIONS

The business owner and the accountant should discuss the financial objectives of the business and how best to achieve them. For example, if the business wants to minimize its profits the financial statements can be prepared one way, and if the business wants high profits other methods must be used. The criteria for the preparation of financial statements are:

- *Use of statements.* The business needs to decide who will receive copies of the financial statements and what their purposes are.
- *Profitability objectives.* Whether the business wants to minimize or maximize profit.

- *Cost.* The expenses incurred in preparing financial statements, which are determined by both the preparer's fee and the frequency of statements.
- *Types of statements.* The number of different financial statements prepared.
- *Acceptability.* The process of assuring that users of the financial statements can rely upon those statements.

CHAPTER HIGHLIGHT

Financial statements should be constructed to enable management to evaluate the effectiveness, economy, and efficiency of operations.

USE QUESTIONS

To ensure that you make maximum use of your financial statements, you should ask your accountant:

QUESTION: What is the main use of the statement of income and expense?

CONSIDERATIONS: This statement shows the bottom-line profitability of your business, and how you reached that position. The statement can be used to establish a number of additional values, calculated as explained:

- *State the cost of products sold.* Costs deducted from sales to calculate gross profits.
- *Establish product selling price.* If gross or net profit is too low one solution is to increase the selling price.
- *Monitor inventory usage.* Inventory consumption is shown in gross profit calculation.

- *Monitor administrative costs.* Administrative costs are normally totaled and can be compared to gross sales to identify excessive costs.
- *Identify unprofitable areas.* Requires income to be calculated for each product line or product.
- *Identify employee theft.* If profit based on sales is too low it may indicate employee theft.

QUESTION: What are the primary uses of the balance sheet?

CONSIDERATIONS: The balance sheet is designed to show the assets owned by the business, the amount of long- and short-term debt, and the owner's equity. In addition, the balance sheet can be used to:

- Identify the business's ability to pay its bills (a combination of available cash less short-term debt).
- Determine ratios of assets to debts to evaluate whether the business has borrowed too much money, and may have a problem carrying the debt-interest payments.

QUESTION: How can my financial statements be used to identify the profitability of a product or product line?

CONSIDERATIONS: Assuming that the accounting records contain sufficient detail, the statement of income and expense can be expanded to spread revenue and cost of sales over products or product lines. Normally this is done for lines of products in the calculation of gross profit. Costs are distributed by product or product line where known, and by percent of sales when costs cannot be easily divided by product lines. It is important for businesses to do this so they know how much gross profit they are making on each product or product line. Without this type of financial statement, the business may not realize it's selling some products at a loss.

QUESTION: Who should get copies of my financial statements?

CONSIDERATIONS: The primary users of financial statements are the management and owners of the business. If you are in need of a loan the statements should also be made available to your banker. In addition, you will have to provide copies of your financial statements to government agencies such as the Internal Revenue Service.

QUESTION: What type of financial statement do I have to provide to government agencies?

CONSIDERATIONS: The types of financial statements you must prepare for government agencies depends upon the agency to whom you are required to report. The Internal Revenue Service requires only a statement of income and expense and a balance sheet. If, however, you must report to the Securities and Exchange Commission, you may have to prepare a series of unique statements as a means of disclosing information it deems important.

QUESTION: Should I give outside parties all of the financial statements my business prepares?

CONSIDERATIONS: Outside parties usually are only interested in a statement of income and expense and a balance sheet. Other reports prepared for your business would normally not be given others. In addition, you may prepare very detailed statements of income and expense for your own use in managing the company but may not want to give those detailed statements to outside parties. For example, if you spread your revenue and expenses to show the profitability of product lines, you do not want this information in the hands of your competitors.

QUESTION: How long should I save my financial statements?

CONSIDERATIONS: You should save your financial statements from the time you begin business. It is interesting to see trends of business growth and profitability over time and complete records may be influential in proving your growth patterns to banks and potential investors.

QUESTIONS ABOUT TYPES OF STATEMENT

If you are uncertain as to what financial statements you should prepare, ask your accountant:

QUESTION: What financial statements must I prepare for my business?
CONSIDERATIONS: Unless you are a publicly held corporation, the balance sheet, statement of income and expense, and the source and application of funds are the only statements normally prepared. The balance sheet and statement of income and expense are required for tax purposes. Publicly held companies in special industries may be required to prepare other financial statements.
QUESTION: Should I prepare comparative statements of income and expense?
CONSIDERATIONS: Comparative statements show this year's revenue and expenses compared to last year's revenue and expenses. They are helpful in evaluating business operations from one year to the next and give you ratios of expense to revenue. For example, if revenue is down or expenditures are up in one area, it is readily apparent if comparative statements are prepared.
QUESTION: What statements should I prepare in addition to the statement of income and expense and the balance sheet?
CONSIDERATIONS: Most businesses should prepare a cash-flow statement for use in projecting their cash needs or to help in investment planning. Most other financial statements are variations of the statement of income and expense. Whether they are necessary relates to what information you require to manage your business most effectively.
QUESTION: What type of information about my business must be disclosed in addition to financial information?
CONSIDERATIONS: Financial statements must be prepared in accordance with generally accepted accounting procedures. These accounting procedures provide options to businesses in

preparing their statements. Generally the business needs to discuss the options if these are to have a material effect on the financial statements. Normally only publicly held corporations need to make disclosures—and then, only those specified by accounting procedures and government agencies regulating the corporations. For privately held corporations, disclosure is usually necessary only when statements are given to outside parties, such as bankers, for support of a loan request.

QUESTION: How can financial statements indicate which parts of my business are profitable and which are not?

CONSIDERATIONS: Larger businesses may want to prepare statements that differentiate the various business functions into individual profit centers. This approach treats each specialized area, such as marketing or production, as if it were a business itself, responsible for its own profit or loss. That area can then determine how effectively it is being managed.

ACCEPTABILITY QUESTIONS

If you are concerned about the acceptability of your financial statements, you should ask your accountant:

QUESTION: How much reliance should I place on the profit or loss shown on my financial statement?

CONSIDERATIONS: Your statements will vary according to the accounting methods used and thus must be interpreted in light of the accounting options selected. For example, in the Hypothetical Corporation, example B showed a loss that might discourage bankers from lending money or people from investing in the business. What impression you want to create of your business's operations will determine the accounting methods you should use in preparing your financial statements.

QUESTION: Do my financial statements need to be audited or certified by an independent accountant?

CONSIDERATIONS: Unless you are a publicly held corporation or are required to do so by loan agreements, it is probably unnecessary and undesirable to have your statements audited or certified. The purpose of an audit is to provide an independent view of the accuracy of your statement to stockholders and other interested parties.

QUESTION: Do I need to get my financial statement certified?

CONSIDERATIONS: You cannot obtain a certified financial statement unless your business is audited. Once an audit is certified your accountant assumes financial accountability for significant errors in your statements owing to improper auditing procedures. Unless you are a publicly held corporation, it is probably not necessary to have your financial statements certified. Certification requires a prior audit, and that cost has to be weighed against the benefits received.

QUESTION: What can my accountant do to improve the acceptability of my financial statements?

CONSIDERATIONS: Accountants can prepare a "transmittal letter" to accompany your financial statements, which will add credibility to them. This letter is not a certification but states what procedures your accountant performed in analyzing and preparing the statements.

QUESTION: What is the real value of certified financial statements?

CONSIDERATIONS: The value to the bankers and investing public is that the accountant holds himself personally liable, in conjunction with management, for the reasonableness of the financial statements. In other words, if the statements do not fairly reflect the status of the company, then the accountant can be sued by a damaged party.

CHAPTER 14
Putting It All Together

A MERCHANT with a small business in a desirable location was doing an excellent business. Things looked promising until one day the merchant noticed a sign proclaiming that a major department store was opening a huge facility on the next lot. The merchant's despair grew deeper when a sign on the other side of his small shop indicated another large department store was also opening a store. Nestled between two giants the small merchant saw little opportunity to continue in business. After extensive thought, however, the merchant hit upon an idea to salvage his business. On the day of the grand opening of the two department stores, with their banners flying, the small merchant—nestled in the center—erected a huge sign over his store with the words, "Main Entrance."

You may wonder at times whether being in business is worth it. There is a time for profit, a time for customer complaints, a time for employee uprising, and a time for the pleasures of ownership. Every so often the owner of the business should assess the viability of the business, its long-range potential, and his own desire to continue. Most of the energy and effort of a business must go into the day-to-day battle for survival. The bottom line reflects the profits for this month or this year. Plans and strategies deal with ordering supplies for tomorrow, hiring competent people, and convincing enough customers to buy your service or products to survive. This leaves little time for long-term self-analysis.

Yet this periodic reassessment is healthy for the business—even if painful for the individual conducting the assessment. The results of such an assessment can lead to positive business changes that increase profitability and make the business more challenging to the owners. And it is in terms of financial analysis that your accountant becomes important to you. The questions you need to answer in this large-scale strategic analysis are:

- Is my business in a growth industry?
- Will my company be able to capitalize on that growth, or suffer because of declining segments of a related business?
- Is my business financed and structured well enough to compete with my competitors?
- Will my industry be rapidly changing, and if so, will it be able to survive the changes?

The answers to these questions can be obtained through a financial analysis of your business and your industry similar to those on publicly held corporations made by stockbrokers. Step away from your business and analyze it as an outside investor might, basing your conclusions solely on fact, not on emotions. The end result of the analysis will be a self-administered recommendation to buy, sell, or hold. A buy conclusion indicates a prosperous future, a sell conclusion a gloomy one. A hold recommendation indicates a period of stagnation unless an action plan is developed to improve the business situation.

Your analysis should be two-fold: first, a static analysis to show where your business stands; second, a comparison of your business against industry norms.

STATIC ANALYSIS

The type of static analysis you should perform includes:

- *Return on invested capital.* The percent of net profit you are getting on the money you invested in your business. For example if you invested $150,000 in your business and earned $50,000 this year, your return on invested capital would be 33⅓ percent.
- *Inventory turnover.* The number of times you are able to sell your inventory during the year.
- *Owner's hourly wage.* The profits, divided by the hours the owners work gives the owner's hourly wage.
- *The rate of growth and direction of sales change.* Sales change over five years, expressed as percent of first year.
- *The rate of growth and direction of profit change.* Profit change over five years, expressed as percent of first year.
- *Other analyses.* Other analyses unique to your industry or business.

COMPARATIVE ANALYSIS

You should evaluate your relative position in your industry as follows:

- Sales as a percentage of investment versus industry norm.
- Business's percentage of profit versus industry norm.
- Business's return on investment versus industry norm.
- Employees' salaries as a percentage of sales versus industry norm.
- Business's percentage growth in sales versus industry norm.
- Business's percentage growth in profit versus industry norm.
- Other comparisons as required to help assess the business.

WHERE DO I GO FROM HERE?

The financial analysis will indicate the status of your business's financial health and how it stacks up against the industry's. As a comparison, you may wish to build a profile showing your variation from the industry norm. Such a chart generally proves helpful in making adjustments in business strategy. A business-comparison profile is illustrated in Figure 9, which uses the comparative indicators discussed in this chapter. The bars going up or down from the norm line show the percent of variation between this business and the industry norm. For example, the chart shows that the Hypothetical Corporation made 5 percent more sales than the average business in its industry but 10 percent less profit on those sales. The chart shows that the company spent 6 percent more on employee salaries as a percent of sales than the industry and received 2 percent less return on investment than the industry norm. This analysis would tell the business it is less profitable than the norm, probably because it is spending too much on salaries. The analysis should cause the business to reassess either the number of employees it has or the salary paid those employees.

Knowing this information is not enough. *Acting* on the information is crucial. The success of the good franchises lies in the fact that the franchiser performs many of these analyses and helps the individual franchisee develop an action plan on the basis of the results.

The nonfranchisee does not have this expert help readily available and must look to other sources for assistance. One good source of help is the business's accountant, who can help perform the various analyses and work with the business's owners or managers to provide the necessary action plan.

The business analysis provides a diagnosis of the health of the business. The action plan is the prescription to cure any illnesses detected during the examination. Assuming a problem has been detected, the owner can select one of the following plans of action or inaction:

Figure 9

Business Comparison Profile as of December 31, 19XX

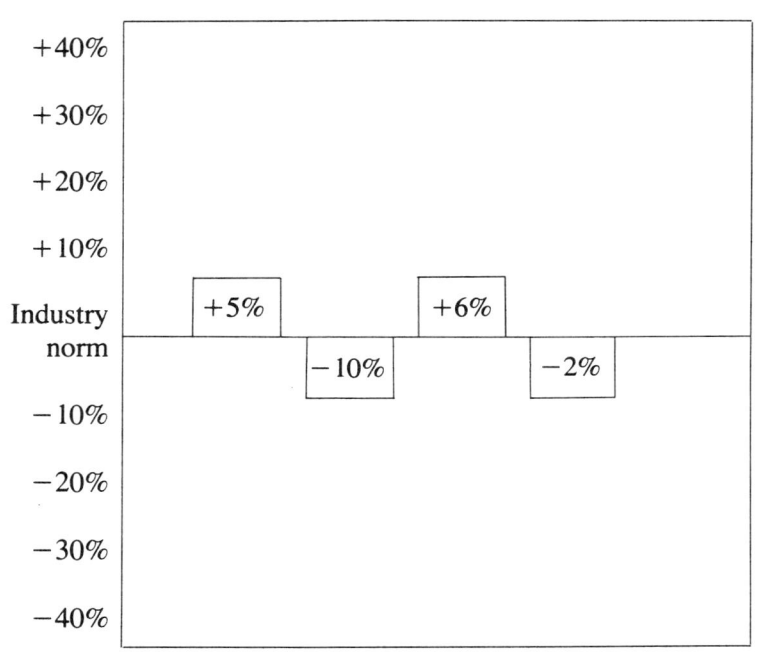

	Sales as a percent of investment	Profit on sales	Salaries as a percent of sales	Return on investment
Variance from industry norm	+5%	−10%	+6%	−2%

- *Do nothing.* The owner may not be prepared to address the problem at this time or does not believe the problem warrants action.
- *Evaluate the symptoms and recommend a solution.* The owner or other skilled people can evaluate the situation and recommend the best solution. Frequently the problem itself suggests the solution. For example, if the business's inventory turnover is considerably less than the industry average, the business needs to reassess its inventory policy to determine whether or not it is losing investment revenue or paying excessive interest through overstocking.
- *Eliminate the problem.* Remove the cause of the problem: sell off an unprofitable branch, drop an unprofitable line of business, or fire a troublesome employee.

IS THERE ANYBODY BESIDES MY ACCOUNTANT?

Accountants know accounting and normally are well qualified to advise you on financial matters. However, when the accountant steps outside of his traditional role, the advice he gives may be that of the average man on the street. In other words, if your accountant advises you on how to design an advertising campaign, the advice may be based on the accountant's individual lay opinion, not expertise.

A successful business builds a staff of technical consultants, of whom the accountant is just one, albeit often one of the more trusted and relied upon. Because of the relationship of trust binding you, your business, and your accountant, he may know more about your business than any other individual besides yourself. Rely on his advice—but not to the exclusion of other consultants you have access to.

The consultants (in addition to your accountant) you should consider adding to the staff are discussed below.

Legal counsel. Your business should engage the services of a legal firm. It is normally to your advantage to work with an individual lawyer so you can call this person whenever necessary. Unless you have a close working relationship with an attorney, you will be hesitant about calling him in on many day-to-day situations that might result in some serious legal problem. Many businesses engage a legal firm on a retainer basis, which means that they pay the legal firm a fixed fee per year for the privilege of representation. The retainer rarely exceeds $250 to $500 per year and enables you to call the firm periodically at no additional charge to gain legal advice.

Insurance/financial advisor. You should work with an insurance agent who is a trained financial advisor. This particular individual is expert in business insurance, including medical plans, health plans, and business life-insurance plans. The individual should also be qualified in the tax implications of benefit plans. The proper insurance financial advisor can help you create tax shelters and avoid taxes by establishing the most advantageous benefit programs. Usually you pay no fee for these services and are not obligated to purchase insurance from these advisors unless they can convince you of the value of their plan.

Investment counselor. Many firms specialize in helping to invest your funds in real estate partnerships, stocks and bonds, financing new businesses, and so on. These investment counselors usually specialize in working with businesses or groups of individuals to select good investments, manage them, and liquidate them at the appropriate time. If you choose to invest with these firms, there is generally a fee, which may be part of the investment, a commission on the purchase or sale of the investment, or a management fee. However, until you actually make an investment there is normally no fee for their advice and recommendations.

Stockbroker. A member of a brokerage firm who buys and sells investments handled by the brokerage firm.

Business-equipment marketing representative. The representatives of the vendors of equipment used in your business will work with you in selecting, installing, and showing you how to best utilize their equipment. If these marketing representatives are good, they will help you install equipment that will improve the efficiency and profitability of your business. You should expect them to analyze your business and demonstrate how their product will help increase its profitability. There is normally no fee for this service, as the goal is to sell you a product. You may want to work with marketing representatives of several different vendors.

Forms/supplies marketing representatives. These individuals provide the equivalent services for their products as the equipment marketing representatives.

PUTTING IT ALL TOGETHER

Sit back and enjoy your business until a cold, snowy midwinter evening. Then pack up your cares and fly to Florida with your accountant on a tax-deductible junket. Lie on the soft sands of Ft. Lauderdale and agonize with your accountant over whether it is worth it to endure the hardships of business ownership.

As you evaluate your business and attempt to put it all together, consider:

- *Am I making it?* Analyze the financial health of your business.
- *Do I need help?* If all is not as rosy as it should be, can I get out of the mess by myself, or am I in over my head and do I need help to climb out of the hole I have dug for myself?
- *Where do I get help?* Whom should I turn to for the solutions to my problems?

CHAPTER HIGHLIGHT

An occasional analysis of your business indicates whether you're traveling on the right road to success.

AM I MAKING IT?

If you want to know the financial health of your business, you should ask your accountant:

QUESTION: Is my business making maximum use of its resources?
CONSIDERATIONS: You have invested resources in your business, and an analysis of your investments can tell you how effectively resources are being utilized. For example, would you be better off putting your money in a savings bank certificate of deposit than investing your funds in your business? This type of analysis will show whether you are receiving a fair return for your time and invested funds.
QUESTION: Is my business considered successful in its industry?
CONSIDERATIONS: One measure of success is your business's performance versus that of other similar businesses. You may feel successful when you analyze the results of your operations, but if, when those results are compared against the industry averages, you find you rank near the bottom you may want to reconsider some of your business policies.
QUESTION: How can I compare the success of my business against industry averages?
CONSIDERATIONS: Many groups study different industries and publish statistics about them. Sometimes you can get these industry statistics from the federal government. One good source is the U.S. Department of Commerce. Industries that have trade associations frequently publish statistics for the

benefit of their members. If none of these sources is available, your accountant may be able to put you in contact with one or more of your competitors so you can form a miniassociation to help one another.

QUESTION: How can I find out whether there is a trade associaition for my industry?

CONSIDERATIONS: If your accountant specializes in your industry, he should know. If your accountant cannot help you, your local Chamber of Commerce should be able to tell you whether or not there is an appropriate trade association.

QUESTION: Whom should I engage to perform a management analysis of my business?

CONSIDERATIONS: Your accountant is an obvious candidate to perform this analysis. However, your accountant should be continually advising you on the financial health of your business in any event. If your accountant has not been doing this it may be because he is not experienced in such a management analysis. If not, you may wish to engage another accounting firm, particularly a national company that should have an expert in your industry, or hire an independent consultant who specializes in your industry.

QUESTION: What types of management analyses should I perform on my business?

CONSIDERATIONS: The types of management analyses that have been most successful are done by franchisers. These examinations are performed by experienced individuals knowledgeable in the business. The analyses review marketing, production, advertising, image of business locations, and other aspects of the business. Through the Chamber of Commerce or mutual friends you should examine the financial statements prepared by and for franchisees and evaluate the type of analysis and information given franchisees by their franchisers. Determine if this kind of analysis is applicable to your business.

DO I NEED HELP?

If you feel you may need help to improve your business, ask your accountant:

QUESTION: How can I tell when it is necessary to perform a management analysis?
CONSIDERATIONS: If you answer yes to one of the following questions:

- Are your business profits falling?
- Have you lost interest in your business?
- Is the number of your competitors increasing, or are they becoming more aggressive?
- Has there been a significant change in your industry recently (e.g., new methods of performing work)?

QUESTION: If an analysis is called for, when should it be performed?
CONSIDERATIONS: As soon as possible, but not during a busy period for your business.
QUESTION: How frequently should these analyses be undertaken?
CONSIDERATIONS: It would be unusual to benefit from a management review if one has been conducted during the past two years unless some unusual event had occurred—such as hiring a new president.

WHERE DO I GET HELP?

If you need skills not available in your own business, you should ask your accountant:

QUESTION: What services in addition to accounting does your firm perform?
CONSIDERATIONS: The types of additional services that accounting firms commonly perform include:

- Tax services.
- Audits.
- Security and Exchange Commission report preparation.
- Business consulting.
- Computer selection studies.
- Computer system development.
- Computer service center facilities.

In addition, some accounting firms specialize in certain industries. In Florida, some CPA firms specialize in the citrus-fruit industry, in Kentucky the horse-breeding industry, and in Iowa, farming. If you have some unique industrial problems, you should look for a firm that specializes in your industry.

QUESTION: What legal firms would you recommend that my business engage?

CONSIDERATIONS: Just as you would ask your lawyer who are the better accountants, you should ask your accountant who are the better lawyers. While your accountant may not recommend a specific firm, he probably has had experience with many in your area and may be able to recommend the better-qualified companies, especially the names of individual lawyers with whom you might work.

QUESTION: Whom would you recommend as an investment counselor?

CONSIDERATIONS: Many investment schemes are evaluated by accountants. Your accounting firm may have personal experience working with investment counselors and therefore may be in a good position to recommend someone to you.

QUESTION: Whom would you recommend as a stockbroker?

CONSIDERATIONS: Accountants are usually in regular contact with lawyers and investment counselors doing financial analyses for them, but they may not have the same close working relationship with a stockbroker. However, accountants work with many individuals who invest in stocks, and so your accountant may be able to make a good recommendation to you for a stockbroker.

QUESTION: Whom would you recommend as an insurance-investment analyst?

CONSIDERATIONS: Most businesses work with an insurance analyst in putting together pension plans, insurance programs, and so on. Because of the tax implications of many of these plans, investment counselors work with accounting firms. Your accountant may be able to recommend a qualified insurance-investment analyst.

QUESTION: If my business should need equipment, forms, or supplies, whom would you recommend that I contact regarding my needs?

CONSIDERATIONS: The accounting firm may have the same requirements as to your business for equipment, forms, and supplies. In addition, accountants visit other clients regularly who also require these services. Your accountant's recommendations may help you find the best suppliers of such items.

BOOK HIGHLIGHT

A good accountant can be a full service resource for your business—use that resource to your best advantage.

Appendix

SMALL-BUSINESS REFERENCES

- Associations
- Government Agencies
- Magazines
- Books
- Bulletins, Reports, and Newsletters

Associations

American Association of Small Business or National Small
Business Association
1604 K St., NW
Washington, D.C. 20006

> 50,000 members. Provides information on the development of an independent small business.

American Federation of Small Business
407 S. Dearborn St.
Chicago, Illinois 60605

> 5,000 members. Provides information on pending state and federal legislation.

International Council for Small Business
c/o Robert O. Bauer
University of Wisconsin Extension
929 N. Sixth St.
Milwaukee, Wisconsin 53203

> 800 members. Undertakes research on the development of small-business management.

National Association of Small-Business Investment Companies
618 Washington Bldg.
Washington, D.C. 20005

> 450 members. Holds executive-training seminars.

Conference of American Small-Business Organizations
407 S. Dearborn St.
Chicago, Illinois 60605

> Provides information on the defense of the free-market economy.

National Federation of Independent Business
150 W. Twentieth Ave.
San Mateo, California 94403

> 620,000 members. Presents small-business viewpoints to state and national legislative bodies.

Government Agencies

Small Business Administration
1441 L Street, NW
Washington, D.C. 20416

Departments

> Office of Equal Employment Opportunity and Compliance
> Counsel for Advocacy
> Size Appeals Board
> Office of Hearings and Appeals
> Congressional and Legislative Affairs
> National Advisory Council

Programs

> Financial Assistance
> Procurement Assistance
> Management Assistance
> Investment

Women's Business Enterprise
Minority Small Business and Capital Ownership Development
Capital Ownership Development
Business Development
Policy, Planning and Budgeting
Controller
Industry Analysis Division
Policy Analysis and Review Division
Support Services
Field Services
Personnel Management Division
Data and Management Services Division
Public Communication Division
Office of Advocacy
Interagency Policy Division
Economic Research Division
Information/Organization Division
Small Business Services Management Division

Magazines for Small Businesses

Catalog of United States Government Publications.
> U.S. Government Printing Office, Washington, D.C. 20402
> Source of federal government publications issued monthly by the Superintendent of Documents.
>
> Subject, author, and title index

Small Business Management
 ICP Inc.
 9000 Keystone Crossing
 Indianapolis, Indiana 46240

 Software and data services

Small Business News
 Federal Business Development Bank
 360 St. Jacques
 Montreal, Quebec, Canada H3H 129

Small Business News
 Smaller Business Association of New England
 69 Hickory Dr.
 Waltham, Massachusetts 02154

 Management aids

Small Business Newsletter
 7514 North 53rd Street
 Milwaukee, Wisconsin, 53223

Inc.
 Inc. Publishing Company
 38 Commercial Wharf
 Boston, Massachusetts 02110

Small Business Report
 Northrop Corp., Aircraft Group
 1800 Century Park E.
 Century City, Los Angeles, California 90067

Small Business Reporter: Financing Small Business
 Bank of America
 Box 3700
 San Francisco, California 94137

Small Business Research Series
   U.S. Small Business Administration
   Superintendent of Documents
   Government Printing Office
   Washington, D.C. 20402

Small Business, Select Committee
   Annual Report
   Washington, D.C. 20510

Small Businessman's Clinic
   c/o Austin Elliot
   113 Vista del Lago
   Scotts Valley, California 95066

Small Industry Development Network Quarterly Newsletter
   Industrial Development Division
   Georgia Institute of Technology
   Atlanta, Georgia 30332

Books About Small Businesses

SELECTING AND STARTING

Be Free: Happiness Is Owning Your Own Business. Robert Haisman. New York: Simon and Schuster, 1980.
402 Things You Must Know Before Starting Your Own Business. Philip Fox. Englewood Cliffs, N.J.: Prentice-Hall, 1980.
Guide To Buying, Selling, and Starting A Travel Agency. Laurence Stevens. Merton, 1976.

How to be Your Own Boss: The Complete Handbook of Starting and Running a Small Business. Walter Szykitka, ed. New York: New American Library, 1978

How to Buy, Sell and Finance a Business. Stanley Mattox. Mattox, 1977.

How to Form Your Own Corporation Without a Lawyer. Rev. ed. Ted Nicholas. Wilmington, Delaware: Enterprise, 1977.

How to Make Big Profits in Service Businesses. Scott Witt. Englewood Cliffs, N.J.: Parker, 1977.

How to Make Money in Your Kitchen. Jeffrey Feinman. New York: William Morrow, 1977.

How to Make Up to $100 an Hour Every Hour You Work. John Stockwell. Englewood Cliffs, N.J.: Parker, 1979.

How to Pick the Right Small Business Opportunity. Kenneth Albert. New York; McGraw-Hill, 1980.

How to Pyramid Small Business Ventures into a Personal Fortune. Mark Stevens. Englewood Cliffs, N.J.: Parker, 1977.

How to Start, Finance and Manage Your Own Small Business. Joseph Mancuso. Englewood Cliffs, N.J.: Prentice-Hall, 1978.

How to Start Your Own Business. J.K. Lasser Tax Institute. New York: Simon and Schuster, 1980.

How to Win the Battle Against Inflation with a Small Business. Murray Miller. Wilmington, Delaware: Enterprise, 1980.

Inc. Yourself: How to Profit by Setting Up Your Own Corporation. Judith McQuown. New York: Macmillan, 1980.

How to Start Your Own Craft Business. Herb Genfen. New York: Watson-Guptill, 1974.

How to Start Your Own Small Business. Drake, 1979.

How to Turn Your Ideas into a Million Dollars. Don Kracke. New York: Doubleday, 1977.

Mother Earth News Handbook on Home Business Ideas and Plans. Mother Earth News Staff. New York: Bantam, 1976.

Small-Time Operator. Bernard Kamoroff. Bell Springs, 1977.

Woman's Guide to Starting a Business. Rev. ed. New York: Holt, Rinehart, 1980.

Working for Yourself: How to be Successfully Self-Employed. Geoff Hewitt. Emmaus, Pa.: Rodale, 1978.

FINANCING

Business Loans: A Guide to Money Sources and How to Approach Them Successfully. Rick Hayes. Boston, Mass.: CBI, 1980.

Corporate Finance Sourcebook. Rick Hayes. Boston, Mass.: CBI, 1980.

Entrepreneurship and Venture Management. Clifford Baumback. Englewood Cliffs, N.J.: Prentice-Hall, 1975.

Financing Business Firms sixth ed. James Wert. Homewood, Ill.: Richard D. Irwin, 1979.

Guide to Venture Capital Sources Fourth ed. Stanley Rubel. Capital, 1977.

Handbook of Business, Finance and Capital Sources. Dileep Rao. New York: Amacom, 1980.

How Public Financing Can Help Your Company Grow Fifth rev. ed. Maxwell Mangold. New York: Pilot Industries, 1975.

How to Finance Your Small Business With Government Money: SBA Loans. Rick Hayes. New York: Wiley, 1980.

Where the Money is and How to Get It. Ted Nicholas. Wilmington, Del.: Enterprise, 1976.

Complete Guide to Making a Public Stock Offering. Elmer L. Winter. Englewood Cliffs, N.J.: Prentice-Hall, 1972.

Why, When, and How to Go Public. George Scott Hutchinson. New York: Presidents Publishing House, 1970.

How and Where to Raise Venture Capital to Finance a Business. Ted Nicholas. Wilmington, Del.: Enterprise, 1976.

How to Become Financially Successful. Albert Lowry. New York: Simon and Schuster, 1981.

MANAGING

Accounting, Finance, and Taxation: A Basic Guide for Small Business. C. Richard Baker. Boston, Mass.: CBI, 1979.

Basic Book of Business. John Klug. Cahners, 1977.

Compensating Key Executives in the Smaller Company. Theodore Cohn. New York: Amacom, 1979.

Computerize Your Small Business Spectrum. Jules Cohen. Englewood Cliffs, N.J.: Prentice-Hall, 1980.

Computers and Information Systems in Business. George Brabb. Boston, Mass.: Houghton-Mifflin, 1980.

Entrepreneur's Manual: Business Start-Ups, Spin-Offs and Innovative Management. Richard White. Radnor, Pa.: Chilton, 1977.

Entrepreneurship and Small Business Management. Hans Schollhammer. New York: Wiley, 1979.

Help! There's a Computer in the Office. Carl Goldman. Rising Star, 1979.

How to Buy and Sell a Small Business. Drake, 1975.

How to Do Your Own Accounting for a Small Business. Robert Milliron. Wilmington, Del.: Enterprise, 1980.

How to Organize and Operate a Small Business Sixth ed. Clifford Baumback. Englewood Cliffs, N.J.: Prentice-Hall, 1980.

How to Run a Small Business. J.K. Lasser Institute. New York: McGraw-Hill, 1974.

Introduction to Data Processing for Business. Robert Thierauf. New York: Wiley, 1979.

Managing the Survival of Smaller Companies. Arthur Hazel. Plano, Texas: Business Books, 1973.

Practical Accounting for Small Businesses. Lyn Taetzsch. Princeton, N.J.: Petrocelli/Charter, 1977.

Practical Bookkeeping for the Small Business. Mary Dyer. Chicago, Ill.: Contemporary Books, 1976.

Running Your Own Business. Howard Stern. New York: Crown, 1980.

Small Business: Developing the Winning Management Team. George Rimler. New York: Amacom, 1980.

Small Business Management Fourth ed. Halsey Broom. SW, 1975.

Small Business Management Fundamentals. Dan Steinhoff. New York: McGraw-Hill, 1974.

Successful Small Business Management. Curtis Tate. Plano, Texas: Business Publications, 1975.

Successful Small Business Management. Leon Wortman. New York: Amacom, 1976.

Tax Guide for Small Business. U.S. Bureau of Internal Revenue.

ADVERTISING AND MARKETING

Advertising and Promoting the Professional Practice. Morton Walker. New York: Hawthorn, 1979.

Advertising for a Small Business. Jeffrey Feinman. New York: Simon and Schuster, Cornerstone, 1980.

All You Ever Wanted to Know About Advertising. Gordon Lewis. Chicago, Ill.: Nelson-Hall, 1979.

Do-It-Yourself Marketing Research. George Breen. New York: McGraw-Hill, 1977.

How to Advertise: A Handbook for the Small Business. Sandra Dean. Wilmington, Del.: Enterprise, 1980.

How to Make Your Advertising Twice as Effective. Gordon Lewis. Chicago, Ill.: Nelson-Hall, 1979.

Successful Marketing and Your Small Business. William Brannen. Englewood Cliffs, N.J.: Prentice-Hall, 1978.

BULLETINS, REPORTS, NEWSLETTERS

The Pitfalls in Managing a Small Business
Dun and Bradstreet, Inc. 1977.

Directory for Information and Assistance from Small Business Development Centers
Florida Small Business Development Institute, University of West Florida. Gives sources of information for management assistance for small businesses. State of Florida.

Small Business Reporter
Free from any Bank of America branch, or order from
Bank of America
Dept. 3120, P.O. Box 37,000
San Francisco, California 94137

(*Note*: Small Business Administration has numerous publications on management of small businesses.)

Incorporating a Small Business
Office of General Counsel, Small Business Administration, Management Aids #223
Washington, D.C.
Free from Small Business Administration.

The Federal Wage-Hour Law in Small Firms
Small Business Administration, Small Market Aids #132.

Small Business Report
497 Lighthouse Avenue
Monterey, California 93940

The Future of Small Business in America
Committee on Small Business
House of Representatives, 96th Congress, 1979.
Can be obtained from Government Printing Office, Washington, D.C. 20402

Women's Handbook: How SBA Can Help You Get into Business
Office of Management Assistance
Small Business Administration, 1979.

Checklist for Going into Business
Small Business Administration, 1977.

Small Business and Small Business People
"Vital Issues"—Vol. XXVIII, Number 10
The Center for Information on America
Washington, Connecticut 06793

Starting and Managing a Small Business of Your Own
"The Starting and Managing Series"—Vol. I
Small Business Administration, 1973.